Advance Praise

I have known John Allen for over 20 years; I can confidently say he's a virtuoso at unraveling the seemingly unsolvable. *Simple Strategies* is a master class in problem-solving and brilliantly captures his science-driven, physics-rooted methodology. I've personally witnessed John dissect and resolve issues I believed were impossible. His structured approach has consistently brought clarity and solutions to my most vexing challenges. This book is a must-read for anyone tackling complexity in engineering and beyond.

—**JOE SULLIVAN**, *Former Senior Vice-President, world-wide operations Logitech*

This book succinctly teaches you how to find the basis of unintended performance. Mastering this technique will allow you to quickly solve problems in machine behavior. The model that John Allen presents here is about how to change your mental model of machine behavior to learn something new each day. I encourage you to start your journey with the techniques and tools found in this book.

—**JUDSON B. ESTES**, *Quality Engineering Instructor, Detroit Diesel Professor, Oakland University*

The engineers and problem solvers in *Simple Strategies* are reminiscent of the inventors in the remarkable Turkish novel *Kitab-ül Hiyel*. Both have a relentless pursuit of understanding in creating and working with mechanisms. Both books share the powerful principle of "seeing with fresh eyes" and the realization that all knowledge, no matter how expansive, converges into a single point of clarity – a moment when everything aligns and the solution becomes unmistakable. As a Turkish engineer collaborating with John, I've seen how these principles enable us to diagnose performance and solve technical problems with clarity and efficiency. John's insight and ability to refine this approach are inspiring, and his contributions continue to enhance how we achieve results.

—**ÖZGE EROL**, *Associate Consultant at Crossover Solutions*

A must-read to enable quick problem solving in the most pragmatic manner in industries. Forget half of what you learned on problem solving so far, and you will speed up by a factor of 10.

—DR. GUNTRAM HAAS, *Global Operations Director at MAHLE*

John Allen is an exceptional problem solver who has solved some of the toughest problems. In his new book, he has taken problem solving to the next level with a model-based approach. For any technical problem solver, reading, learning and applying the concepts in this book will be extremely helpful.

—**KUSH SHAH,** *CEO, Global Organizational Excellence Solutions, Six Sigma MBB, DFSS MBB, Shainin Red X Master*

I really enjoyed *Simple Strategies*. The storytelling approach that the author uses is an effective way to understand key concepts like System Behavior and Dynamic Learning. The book offers a wealth of knowledge, presented in a relaxed, conversational tone that makes it enjoyable rather than overwhelming. It's a must-read for problem solvers looking to broaden their skills. This book is also an opportunity to get to know John, not just as an author, but as a person. His personal insights and relatable approach made the learning experience even more enriching.

—**LUIS LOPEZ SANDOVAL,** *Director-Regional Problem Solving Coach, Robert Bosch Automotive Steering LLC*

John reveals the recipe for solving tough problems in design and manufacturing efficiently through engaging and insightful stories. I encourage all problem solvers and leaders to read this book to shift their perspective toward searching for the right questions instead of struggling to find the right answers.

—**RÜYA DEMIRTAŞ,** *Problem Solving Manager, Power Solutions, Bosch*

This is the book that I wish John could have given to me when I first met him decades ago. His passion for Effective Problem Solving shines through these pages. If you have not yet been exposed to John's work and body of knowledge, read this book, then put these strategies and principles to the test. You will not be disappointed, and you will no doubt find that you had a bit of fun along the way!

—**DAVID KNEISLER,** *Vice President of Global Quality, Dana Inc. (Retired) and former Chairman of the Board, Automotive Industry Action Group (AIAG)*

The teachings in John's book have not only allowed us to solve difficult technical problems in days rather than months, but have also reignited our passion for engineering! Jon's approach is a refreshing departure from the conventional "lean-six sigma" black box models, encouraging engineers and technicians to focus not just on solving problems, but on truly understanding the underlying physical principles at play. His inspiring methods make the learning process enjoyable, and the resulting happy customers and significant cost savings are the icing on the cake!

—**BRYAN ZIEGLER,** *Michelin Tire, Operations Director*

Simple Strategies brilliantly blends powerful heuristics, actionable tools, and swashbuckling storytelling. If you work with people, systems, and challenges—and if you are a human being, you do—then you will benefit from reading this revelatory book.

—**HENRY BOWLES,** *PhD, Professional Speaker and Academic*

Simple Strategies

Simple Strategies

A Model-Based Guide to Solving Complex Problems

JOHN ALLEN

NAPLES, FL

Copyright © 2025 by John Allen
All rights reserved.

Published in the United States by
O'Leary Publishing

www.olearypublishing.com

The views, information, or opinions expressed in this book are solely those of the authors involved and do not necessarily represent those of O'Leary Publishing, LLC.

The author has made every effort possible to ensure the accuracy of the information presented in this book. However, the information herein is sold without warranty, either expressed or implied. Neither the author, publisher, nor any dealer or distributor of this book will be held liable for any damages caused either directly or indirectly by the instructions or information contained in this book. You are encouraged to seek professional advice before taking any action mentioned herein.

All rights reserved. No part of this book may be reproduced or transmitted in any form by any means, electronic, mechanical, photocopy, recording, or other without the prior and express written permission of the author, except for brief cited quotes.

For information on wholesale orders or getting permission for reprints and excerpts, contact: O'Leary Publishing at admin@olearypublishing.com.

ISBN: 978-1-952491-86-3 (paperback)
ISBN: 978-1-952491-92-4 (hardcover)
ISBN: 978-1-952491-87-0 (ebook)
Library of Congress Control Number: 2024919770

Developmental Editing by Heather Davis Desrocher
Line Editing by Kat Langenheim
Proofreading David Aretha
Cover and interior design by Jessica Angerstein
Printed in the United States of America

To the many technicians and engineers
from around the world
who I have worked with and learned from.

**Let Crossover Solutions
Solve Your Toughest Problems**

Scan code to visit xosol.com

Contents

List of Tables and Figures xiii

Foreword by David J. Hartshorne and Tobias Mack xvii

Preface – Asking the Right Questions xxi

Introduction – The Principles that Guide Effective Problem Solving 1

Chapter 1 The Power of a Good Model 9

Chapter 2 What Is Happening? 37

Chapter 3 Models and Simplicity 55

Chapter 4 Seeing with Fresh Eyes 73

Chapter 5 Source Load, Effort, and Flow 83

Chapter 6 Expert Knowledge and Dynamic Learning 103

Chapter 7 The Black Box Trap 117

Chapter 8 Structural Decomposition 139

Chapter 9 Models in Life 151

Chapter 10 The Role of Innovation 165

Acknowledgments 173

Appendix 175

Glossary 189

Bibliography 197

About the Author 199

Endnotes 201

List of Figures and Tables

Chapter 1 The Power of a Good Model
Figure 1-1 XO Dynamic Learning 9
Figure 1-2 The Universal Source-Load 11
Table 1-3 Selected Effort-Flow Domains and Conjugates 13
Figure 1-4 Energetic Functions and Properties: 7 x 3 Diagram 14
Figure 1-5 E-FAST Fastener, Contain Potential Energy 19
Figure 1-6 Effort Based Source-Load, Create Clamp Load 20
Figure 1-7 Alternator Rectifier Bridge Cartoon 22
Figure 1-8 E-Fast, Generalized Flow Based 23
Figure 1-9 Cartoon, Cutter Path for Matryoshka 28
Figure 1-10 Small Multiples, Block Machining, Single Cycle 29
Figure 1-11 Multi-vari plot, flawed measurement, multiple time periods, contrast with Small Multiples, one cycle 32
Figure 1-12 Small Multiples, single cycle for a shaft turning operation 33
Figure 1-13 Small Multiples, Brake rotor Machining, single part 34

Chapter 2 What is Happening?
Figure 2-1 Stepper Motor Principles 42
Figure 2-2 Stepper Motor Physics and Logic 43
Figure 2-3 Stepper Motor Cartoon 44
Figure 2-4 Search Tree, "Stuck" Indicator 47
Figure 2-5 Stepper Motor, Direct Measurement of Performance 48
Figure 2-6 Photo or rotor/stator, rotor/magnet, rotor/human finger 49

Chapter 3 Models and Simplicity
Figure 3-1 XO Dynamic Learning Model, the Founding Model 58
Figure 3-2 Cartoon of Coating process, characterising a single cycle 64
Figure 3-3 Small Multiples, cycles and sub-cycles 65
Figure 3-4 Isolation and Separation of INPUTS from FUNCTIONS based on Sparsity of Effects 68

Chapter 4 Seeing with Fresh Eyes

Figure 4-1 Measurment system of coating process that breaks phase with Cycles, sub-cycles 75

Figure 4-2 Integrating the measurment system with the physics of the manufacturing process 76

Figure 4-3 Leaf Spring Cartoon 79

Figure 4-4 Top leaf vs Bottom leaf physics 81

Chapter 5 Source, Load, Effort and Flow

Figure 5-1 Effort-Flow Diagram, Effort Machine: What is Happening as Load and Effort Change 88

Figure 5-2 Effort-Flow Diagram, Flow Machine vs. Effort Machine and consequences 89

Figure 5-3 Flow Machine, Seeing System Impendance, Z 93

Figure 5-4 Mounted, Polished picture, wire severed by bobbin during insertion 95

Figure 5-5 Force in Newtons to insert bobbin and store potential energy (PE) to retain the wire safely 96

Figure 5-6 Insertion force, energy lost to damage wire, not safely stored as PE to retain wire 96

Figure 5-7 Insertion force, energy lost to sever wire, not safely stored as PE to retain wire 97

Figure 5-8 Defining a cycle, Coating Process 99

Figure 5-9 Measurements of Flow and Pressure and two speeds on Effort-Flow Diagram 100

Chapter 6 Expert Knowledge and Dynamic Learning

Figure 6-1 XO Dynamic Learning 108

Figure 6-2 7 Energetic Functions and 3 Properties 113

Chapter 7 The Black Box Trap

Figure 7-1 The Black Box Model 119

Figure 7-2 Regression of a a single variable with scatter from the effects of "the rest" 120

Figure 7-3 XO Dynamic Learning 129

Figure 7-4 Search Tree, Coating Project 131
Figure 7-5 Photo, Coating Project 132
Figure 7-6   Search Tree, updated 133
Figure 7-7 Simplified model, Sparsity of Effects 136
Figure 7-8 Simplified model, Sparsity of Effects 136

Chapter 8 Structural Decomposition
Figure 8-1 XO Roadmap 140
Figure 8-2 The Full Model of Structural Decompostion 144
Figure 8-3 LCD Cartoon 147
Figure 8-4 How Well does zebra strap transmit energy? 149

Figure 10-1 XO Dynamic Learning 172

Appendix
Figure 1 Garage Door 178
Figure 2 Universal Source Load Model 179
Figure 3 Convert Power, Electrical to Rotational 181
Figure 4 Convert Power, Rotational to Translational 182
Figure 5 Effort-Flow Universal Conversion Model 182
Table 6 Selected Domains and Units, SI 183
Figure 7 E-FAST, Grarage Door Opener 184
Figure 8 Tranmit Power, Motor, with Impedance 185
Figure 9 Convert Power, Electrical to Rotational with Units 187
Figure 10 E-FAST with Flow of Power 188

Models are a way of seeing, and better seeing comes from better models. Models summarize, show, and explain something relevant... Models in science and engineering are special because they are based on Nature's forever universal laws, expressed in mathematics describing the physical world. Lacking the guarantee of Nature's mathematical laws, the human sciences are much harder than rocket science... See with fresh eyes. Do not go lazy into default models.

—Edward Tufte

Foreword

by David J. Hartshorne and Tobias Mack,
Partners at Crossover Solutions

If you are involved in the design or manufacture of things, you really should read this book. It goes to the very core of what is required to make engineers, and by extension the companies they work for, extraordinary at what they do. That core is the framework for thinking, or models, that people use to guide their actions: the questions they ask, the observations they make, any data they may use, and the way they organize observations into information that builds knowledge. The most powerful models for understanding System Behavior are ones that simplify the complex in useful ways. These models can be expressed as simple block diagrams and a little text. They represent clarity of thinking. Clarity of thinking – and learning to see with open eyes and constrained by a few principles – is at the heart of this story.

I have been lucky enough to have John as one of my closest friends for over three decades – more than half of my life. We have had countless adventures all over the world both separately and together. We have had the chance to work with many brilliant people. This all came about as a consequence of us choosing to work on, and sharing a passion for, understanding machine performance and reliability – what we call System Behavior. John taught me a great deal over those years; and together we figured out how to learn even more – faster – about the behavior of the huge variety of products and process systems we encountered.

I was fortunate to have participated in some of the moments of insight and inspiration described in this book, and for that I will be forever grateful – and it was a lot of fun. We became efficient and effective at what we did, and as a result, very successful. It was often in situations that seemed impossible to the very talented people who were working ridiculous hours to fix their problems.

Our experience over the years has led to insights that have become principles to which we adhere – no matter what seems to stand in the way. These principles guide the work we do. The illuminating stories in *Simple Strategies* illustrate how a few simple principles allow one to always clearly see System Behavior in a product or manufacturing process. These principles guide us and our clients to quickly solve such problems with the resources at hand while gaining new knowledge, which lies at the center of what we all do.

David J. Hartshorne
London, United Kingdom
Author of *Diagnosing Performance and Reliability*

"A solved problem is always simple and there is always a simple, elegant way to find the answer." I will never forget this statement that John made 32 years ago when we first started working together. We were working on a tough field problem that had been around for years. Five engineering changes did not show any improvement. In fact, the last one seemed to make the problem worse. The team was clearly stuck. John came up with a model to characterize the parts that gave us immediate insight into the failure mechanism. With this model it took us only three days to find the *Causal Explanation* for a problem the experts had worked on for years. Explanation and model both were simple – and it forever changed my view on technical problem solving.

This was the start of a quest for simplicity of which I had the privilege to play a part with my two close friends, John and David, over the last three decades.

It is with great admiration and respect that I invite you to explore John's insights. I have no doubt they will change your view on technical problem solving, like they changed mine 32 years ago.

Enjoy the journey.

Tobias Mack
Munich, Germany

Genius only comes to those who know how to use their eyes and their intelligence.

—Auguste Rodin

Preface

Asking the Right Questions

"Are you having any fun?" I asked a team of eight engineers.

They were surprised by such a question.

"No. We have been working seven days a week for two months," they replied with weariness.

"Do you know more now than you did when you started?" I continued.

It took a while to admit that the answer was "No."

"You thought your job was to find the root cause and solve this problem. For weeks, it has been miserable, and you are no closer to the answer. Maybe we need to change the strategy?"

They were with me to this point.

"First of all, I am not here to solve the problem. I am here to help you learn one thing a day about the physics of *function* and *failed function*. Secondly, I am just here to have a good time."

They looked at me as if they had made a mistake in asking for my help. The *model* they were working under was so flawed that fun was not allowed. At my age, if this were not fun, I would stay home.

My colleagues and I have been helping people just like these frustrated engineers for decades – and what we have learned helps engineers and problem solvers around the world be more efficient and effective. When we shift from failure mode to failed *function*, and stop asking the question *"What is wrong?"* and instead ask *"How well does this work?"* everything changes.

"How well does it work?" is a physics question. *"What's wrong with it?"* relies on expert opinions, and as we have seen, this approach often fails and leaves people frustrated and exhausted.

Solving tough problems is a difficult and often thankless job, made worse if the strategy is flawed. The status quo is to form teams that are too large, and to have Teams meetings or Zoom calls with people around the world at odd hours while pressing for answers and results that never come. Does this sound familiar? You want answers and a solution, but may not really know how to execute a sound progressive search that eliminates where the problem is *not*, or that learns more each day.

The standard problem solving method includes writing problem definitions with a large scope instead of the far more efficient and effective approach of starting with **System Behavior**.[1] It is far more effective to stop focusing on which tool to use and instead use a strategic approach to understand and see the beauty and simplicity of the physical nature of things. You may wonder *how* to do this. This book is here to show you.

Learning has been at the center of my adult life. I have learned from people around the world and in different cultures, and not just from people in the world of science and engineering. **Dynamic Learning** is a choice to change perspective, to see in a fresh way, and it has taught me to ask better questions.

One of the best questions you can ask is: *What do I deserve from the company where I work?* I believe the answer to that question is the following. When you get into your car or on the bus to go home at night, you should feel a measure of satisfaction from learning, knowing more at the end of the day than the start, confident that you are getting closer to a **Causal**

---

[1] Throughout the book there are terms that are capitalized and in bold font. These are terms that are fundamental to the way my colleagues and I think and work.

Explanation[2] for **System Behavior**,[3] and able to make and sell a better product. I do not want you to just fix things, but to also gain new knowledge, because new knowledge is at the heart of innovation. New knowledge is fun, and it is a gift you give to yourself – as well as to the people you work with and the company at which you work.

---

2 For more information see this article: "Root Cause or Causal Explanation" by John Allen, fyx-z.com
3 System behavior is the sum total of a machine's ability to effectively and efficiently perform its intended functions throughout its expected lifetime.

*There is nothing more difficult to take in hand,
more perilous to conduct, or more uncertain in its success,
than to take the lead in the introduction of a new order of
things. For the innovator has enemies in all those who profit
by the old order, and only lukewarmness arising partly from
fear of their adversaries… and partly from the incredulity
of mankind, who do not truly believe in anything new until
they have had the actual experience of it.*

—**Machiavelli**

Introduction

The Principles that Guide Effective Problem Solving

Simple Strategies is the story of innovation, of learning to solve tough technical problems quickly… more quickly than anyone else. It is a story of teaching while learning, of questions and breakthroughs. Hopefully it will offer you a strategic path to solve your toughest problems as it explores what is required to make engineers, and the companies they work for, extraordinary at what they do.

What are the principles that guide success in solving challenging problems? They are the lessons my colleagues and I have learned over many years that make the models (a simple representation of how something works) described in this book powerful. The examples and stories I share are important because they will allow you to follow along with how to see and think in order to develop a strategy and execute it quickly. As you read this book, perhaps you will begin to question the models you have used. This can be a powerful exercise.

Just as importantly, this book contrasts the power of the models my colleagues and I use with others that we have found to be overly complicated and limiting, but have come to structurally dominate industry and problem solving. By the end of this book, I hope you come to believe that perhaps there really is a simpler way to solve your most challenging problems.

What I say might make you uncomfortable at times – but I cannot think of anything in my life that has changed me for the better without a bit of a struggle. If what you are doing is not working as well as you would like it to, you owe it to yourself to explore a different approach that has proven to be successful, or to at least read this book and consider what it has to offer you.

After decades of this work, we have found that you can be a far more effective problem solver when you take a step back, look at the models you are using, challenge them, and be open to a fresh way of seeing. You can improve product performance and reliability if you change the models you use and the questions you ask. Models can guide you, as well as constrain you. Often the models we have in place, both mental and structural, stand in the way. So it is important to adjust or replace flawed models in such a way as to help you see things more quickly and more effectively. This is how you become a better and more effective engineering problem solver.

How can you do this? Over the last 30 years as professional problem solvers, we have developed *10 Principles* that make models more effective. Principles are constraints that keep us focused. They are effective when integrated into your thinking – whether as a leader of a team or when you are working alone. Principles based on models become guides to progress.

The objective is characterizing **System Behavior**. Integrating **Expert Knowledge** and **Dynamic Learning**[1] based on our models leads to innovative solutions that improve product performance and reliability. Here are the principles that guide you.

---

1 **Dynamic Learning** is a strategic process to learn quickly based on **System Behavior** and **Functional Decomposition**.

The 10 Principles of Effective Problem Solving

❶ Models are how we understand and see with fresh eyes.
A model is a simple representation of how something works. Effective models help shape connections, and thus opportunities. Models are how we simplify complexity because we cannot keep all the details of how something works in our brains.

❷ Your job is not to solve the problem. It is to learn.
On the surface, this seems absurd. Of course you have to solve the problem, but how you get there is important. We are often called upon to work with experts where the objective was to solve a problem, but they struggled. That is why we are called. If they have strategically struggled, change the objective! The paradox is that you will figure it out faster when learning is the objective. We have to change the objective to learning.[2]

❸ The objective is to learn one thing every day about the physics of function and failed function.
Changing the objective is important, but we are not interested in *doing a study* – which is a useless endeavor.[3] Studies become passive and tainted; the objective becomes a report instead of a solution. **Dynamic Learning** is not a method for study, but rather a constrained system to learn quickly. Once you are practiced, problems will be solved in days that lingered for months. Learn, and learn every day!

---

[2] I can think back on projects where I thought my own expert knowledge was enough to solve a problem. This fails almost every time for one of two reasons. If I am wrong, I just lost all credibility. Even if I am right, I have set myself into a role of competing against the experts who are part of the team – and no one will learn anything. I tell myself this on every single project! Do not fall into the trap of thinking you have to solve the problem!

[3] I once wrote an article, "Machines Don't Have Issues, Only People Do." https://www.jstor.org/stable/42578601

❹ The fastest route to a Causal Explanation is to characterize System Behavior.
Characterizing **System Behavior** works in conjunction with a progressive search to eliminate where the problem is not. A **Causal Explanation** is a rich description of the answer to the question "What is happening?" Characterizing **System Behavior** is how we go about it.

❺ It is worse than you think!
When a small percentage of failures are reported, the safest assumption is that the reported failures are evidence of a *failed function,* and that all are at risk until proven not to be the case. Focusing on failure modes, although important, will never provide the full story. Characterize **System Behavior**, focus on function, and you will discover the story within the story.

❻ Start with a sample size of one.
Characterizing **System Behavior** with **Source-Load** and **Matryoshka-Small Multiples** develops the important skill of envisioning what has to happen to operate a machine or create one part in one cycle. Often we have been taught to think in terms of large sample sizes. Begin with a **Cartoon**[4] of a single cycle to lay the groundwork for characterizing **System Behavior.**

❼ Thought experiments are devices of the imagination to investigate the nature of things.
Thought experiments are a structured system of deliberation to examine concepts and possibilities without suffering the consequences. Thought experiments are superior to out-of-the-box thinking, which has no constraints. Thought experiments are constrained by **First Principles** of science.

---
4 A Cartoon is a simple sketch to capture manufacturing machine-part interface and datum scheme.

❽ Effective teams consist of two or three people.
More than three people puts a team at risk of becoming a committee. A team accepts responsibility for characterizing **System Behavior** and **Dynamic Learning**, not guessing. Committees hang around the conference room asking theoretical questions instead of learning. Committees multi-task. Teams are focused while committees perpetuate their existence.

❾ Cartooning is the practice of seeing with fresh eyes.
Cartooning is not just drawing a picture on paper but rather learning to draw what you see. The key to cartooning is to actively observe in the lab or on the shop floor, not the conference room. **Cartoons** are developed in the mind, then drawn. It might be most effective to do it on a whiteboard with a marker in one hand and an eraser in the other.

❿ Have fun.
Your professional life is dedicated to making machines run better so customers and employees are safe and the company gains competitive advantage. When you focus on Characterizing **System Behavior** and **Dynamic Learning** instead of problem solving, you will learn more, learn faster, and gain confidence as your skills improve… besides, it is fun. It is our gift to you.

These *10 Principles* will guide you and can transform your problem solving experience. Who are the colleagues with which I have developed these principles? Well, in addition to being a story of innovation and of learning to solve tough technical problems quickly, this book is also a story of friendship. David, Tobias, and I have been working together for over 30 years. I was 41, David, 29, and Tobias was 27 when we first met in Ohio. Although an ocean lies between us, living in Florida, England, and Germany, we are close. No matter the distance, we have become friends – a friendship that began as professional, but has gone well beyond.

Since we met many years ago, we have worked in companies that are familiar to you, and many that are not. We have made significant contributions in the engineering quality sciences, providing those with whom we work the ability to improve product performance and reliability, and to solve problems in days that have lingered, often thinking they were unsolvable. We have helped clients not just solve problems but also make discoveries that led to patents. We share a patent in a power generation system.

We helped a client who makes medical devices for heart patients, and another test equipment for animals. We have worked with most of the automotive companies as well as their suppliers. Our clients make tires and treads for tractors, steering systems, brakes, engines and gearboxes, and now motors and batteries. We have worked on nuclear fuel, electrodes for smelting furnaces, steel mills, casting houses of all kinds, plating companies, injection molding, air bags, food packaging, blow molding, and plastic sheets. The list of products we have worked on for the automobile supply chain has taken us to China, Thailand, India, Korea, Japan, much of Europe, and a few places in the Middle East as well as much of the United States and Mexico. We have gone as far north as the polar circle in Norway, and as far south as Australia and Brazil.

I suppose my reward has been how much I have learned from people who are different from me, their cultures rich and fascinating. Often, I finished a job and did not go home, but rather wandered around cities and jungles, learning from people who see the world in ways that I do not. There was the generosity and care of a driver in India when I was sick, Chinese people in Hangzhou who wanted a picture with an American, and Iranians, whom I met in a lobby and then had dinner with one night, who were selling food processing machines. The children of Laos, who have little, taught me so much with just a smile, especially touching my heart… two of them. I received the Gift of Life, a heart transplant, on September 25, 2017. How I have lived, before and after, and how I see the world of science as well as humanity is part of this story. I hope to weave them together.

Lastly, through all my travels and projects, your culture is at the center. Having seen so much of the world and its cultures, and as an American, I have never once said that you need to change the culture of anything. I know what it means; but I cringe when people say, "We need to change the culture." You might need to *change the way you see*. I hope this book helps you to see with fresh eyes.

I hope you see our legacy as unique, effective, and efficient.

Culture is the name for what people are interested in, their thoughts, their models, the books they read and the speeches they hear.

—Walter Lippman

Models sanctified and celebrated by insiders can evolve into uncontested, lucrative, congealed monopolies/ specialties/cartels/cults/disciplines – which, in time, become self-centered and selfish…

—Edward Tufte

CHAPTER 1

The Power of a Good Model

Everything we do is centered on **System Behavior,** guided by a **Dynamic Learning** process that, at its heart, helps those with a level of technical expertise solve manufacturing and product performance problems quicker.

A system, for our purposes, is any series of linked functions or processes connected to a power supply that results in a desired physical operation or a product containing physical performance characteristics that can be directly sold, or sold to another customer to assemble into another product.

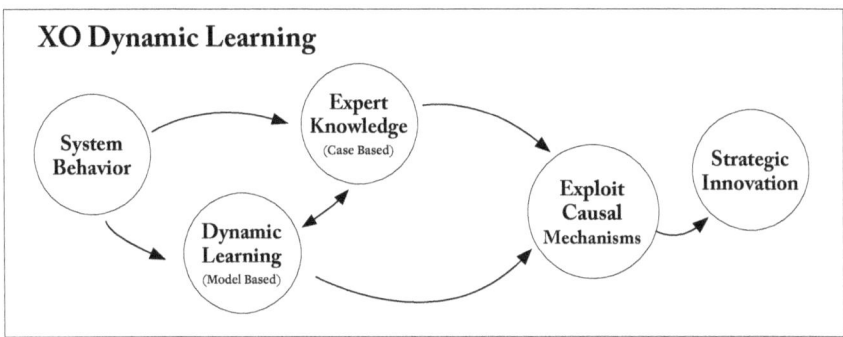

Figure 1-1

We have been guided by the history of science, centered on **First Principles,** which are free of dogma. Time after time experts struggle – but if guided by a means to learn, they can make extraordinary discoveries that lead to innovation and breakthroughs. All we want to do is to show you what we have discovered and tell the fascinating story of how we did it.

To solve tough problems you must have the right model. We have been helping clients solve tough product performance and reliability problems for over 30 years in many industries, companies, and disciplines. Over the course of those years, our pursuit of excellence and drive to constantly see with fresh eyes, questioning and challenging ourselves, as well as our models and principles, has led me to write *Simple Strategies*.

Our models are rigorous and simple, grounded in **First Principles**. Simplicity has an inherent level of beauty that opens pathways to learn.

Primary Models

There are just two primary models for characterizing **System Behavior**:

- The Source-Load Model
- Matryoshka-Small Multiples

There are two secondary models. They are not for characterizing **System Behavior**, but rather to look inside the system as it is characterized. They will be addressed later but the emphasis here is: characterizing **System Behavior** are the primary models.

Much of problem solving today begins with trees of some sort. Trees can be useful if the idea is to solve a problem and move on. Trees are an effective model for convergence based on elimination, but not always the most effective starting point. Characterizing **System Behavior** is grounded in asking, "What is happening?" instead of "What is wrong?" and is the most effective place to start. **Dynamic Learning** leads to innovation and **System Behavior** as a competitive advantage – and solutions that are also simpler and often easier to implement.

Source-Load and **Matryoshka-Small Multiples** are intentionally limited in scope. The scope is limited to provide an effective and simple way to characterize **System Behavior** while maximizing learning.

The Source-Load Model

The **Source-Load** model is a powerful matrix that is an adjunct to hierarchical trees. The nodes of the matrix describe each function with a verb and noun. The verbs and nouns are limited to the small list of energetic functions that describe the serial nature and interdependencies of machine behavior.

Functions are linked by arrows. Arrows are labeled to describe what has to happen to make linked functions work. There is a rigor to identify the functions and nodes and to label the arrows properly to see how energy flows through a machine. Extending the model will be described fully later. Below is the **Universal Source-Load** model. It is useful as a thinking model, and powerful once you learn to describe the **System Behavior** of a machine. Once you learn to use it to characterize **System Behavior** it will become your foundation of quality, performance, and reliability engineering.

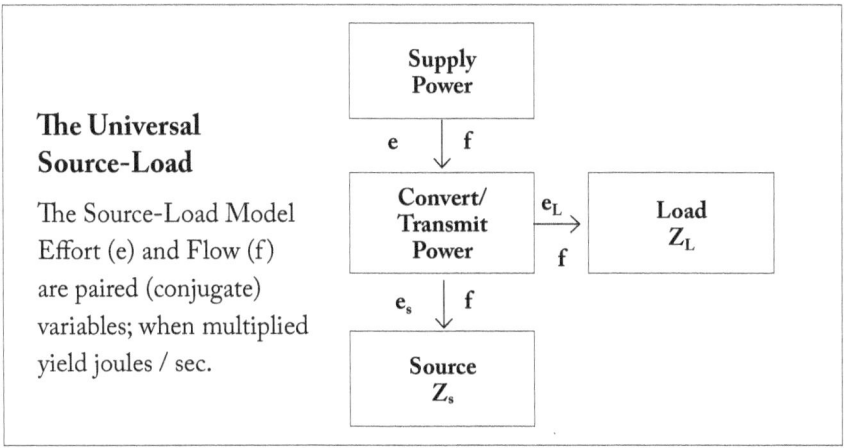

Figure 1-2

Kirchoff's Law and Source-Load

The **Source-Load** model is based on an expanded principle of Kirchhoff's Law, which states that the current entering a junction (node) is equal to the current leaving. If we multiply by voltage, the statement is also true for power entering and leaving. Put another way, if you provide power to a load, the sum of the power to the load from the source plus the losses is zero.

Kirchoff's Law was applied to the electrical domain. We expanded the **Source-Load** model and applied it across domains to provide engineers with the ability to characterize **System Behavior** of machines and expand the model to describe each function as necessary.

Kirchoff's Law is based on current flow. In the electrical domain, if you multiply volts × amps the response is watts, or Joules/second. If we are interested in a rotating shaft, it is called the rotational domain. We can describe its behavior with the angular velocity and the torque. In the hydraulic domain, pressure and volumetric flow describe what is happening. In each case, or each domain, if you multiply the two variables together, the response is watts, or Joules/second. This simple fact of nature provides you with extraordinary leverage in describing **System Behavior**.

We have seen that there are two variables in each domain that are needed to describe the flow of energy, which is called power. The universal language is that one is an effort variable (e), the other the flow variable (f). The flow variable is always the domain-specific units/second. We know that the product of effort × flow is watts regardless of the domain, which provides interesting opportunities to account for losses as energy flows from the source to the load. Performance and reliability engineering must center on characterizing the flow of energy through functions rather than merely time to failure of an entire machine.

Selected Effort-Flow Domains and Conjugates		
Domain	Effort	Flow
Electrical	EMF, V or E	Amps, I
Rotational	Torque, Nm	Radians/sec
Translational	Force	Velocity
Hydraulic	Pressure $N\text{-}m^{-2}$	$m^3 sec^{-1}$

Table 1-3

The most effective way to examine **System Behavior** within or across domains is graphically in the effort-flow workspace – described in detail later – but let's make sure we have a working definition of **System Behavior**.

System Behavior and Source-Load

Once again, **System Behavior**, for our purposes, is any series of linked functions or processes connected to a power supply that results in a desired physical operation, or a product containing physical performance characteristics that can be directly sold, or sold to another customer to assemble into another product.

How can you really claim that quality is important if you do not know how the system behaves that creates it?

Let's have a practical look. Characterizing **System Behavior** is most useful and powerful when limited in scope. It is important to avoid the temptation to create a massive matrix that *includes everything*. You will get unnecessarily frustrated. Our experience is that simple models are far more practical on every level. If you are in a leadership role, remember that the practicality of any model lies in simplicity.

The foundation is always the **Universal Source-Load** model (Figure 1-2). It is expanded only to the extent necessary while adding functions that we may choose to expand later… or not.

The basic building block for the **Source-Load** model is the 7 × 3 diagram. It is fascinating in that there are only seven functions, meaning you can supply power to a machine and then do six more things with that energy across multiple domains.

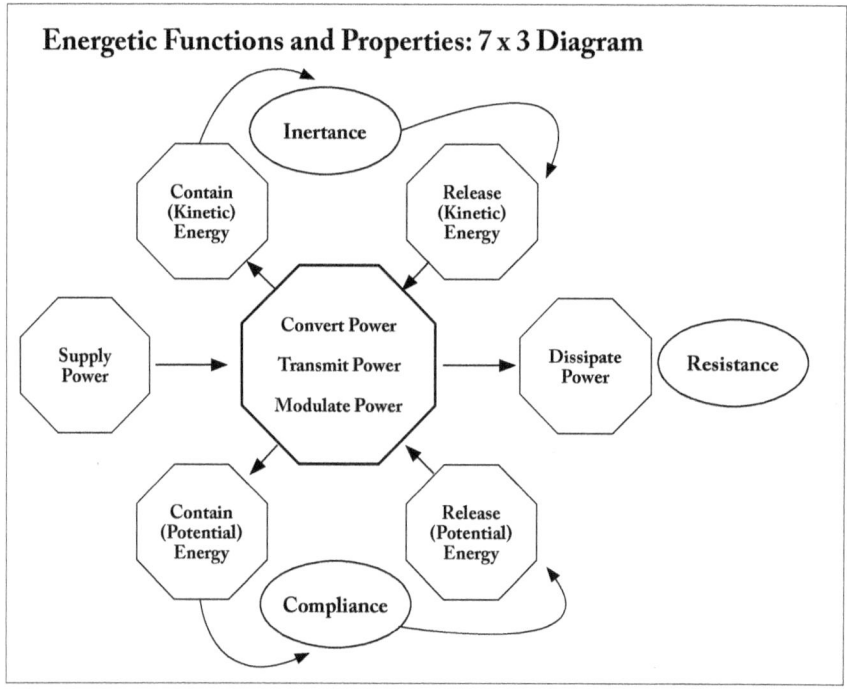

Figure 1-4

The 7 × 3 Diagram shows that you can supply power, move energy from one place to another (transmit), direct or modulate, and convert within a domain (gearboxes) or across domains (electrical to mechanical, etc.). We can contain and release potential and kinetic energy. The properties of interest when we contain and release energy are compliance and inertance. Compliance is the property we care about in things such as springs, bolts, and gaskets. Intertence is the property we are interested in in flywheels and inductors. We can also dampen or dissipate power – sometimes because we want to and sometimes not. Accounting for the difference between the power to the load and that lost to the source provides the answer to an important question: *How well does this work?* The third property we care about as it relates to dampen power is resistance.

Inertance, compliance and resistance are related as they tell the story of impedance.

The beauty of the 7 × 3 Diagram lies in its ultimate simplicity. As we carefully but simply expand the **Source-Load** model, we can see **System Behavior** unfold as it relates to *functions* and *properties* in the 7 × 3 Diagram.

- Why is characterizing System Behavior important? Because it provides:
- Insight and understanding into how things behave
- A universal language based on First Principles and function
- The starting point for FMEA[1], based on failed functions, not failure modes
- A method of test for independent functions before testing at the system level
- A method to account for power losses and energy leaks
- A solid basis for Dynamic Learning
- A single foundation for new product development, validation, performance, and reliability engineering
- And most importantly, it starts by changing the question from *What is wrong?* to *What is happening?* This will simplify and ground your problem-solving strategy.
- Lastly, Source-Load tells the story of machine behavior from data to information, then knowledge.

---

1 Failure Mode and Effects Analysis

There are several examples in the chapters that follow with case stories and applications. The message is always *fundamentals* and *simplicity*. In the stories, you will see how often we were able to help clients solve tough problems quickly. In every case, we started with characterizing **System Behavior**. In many projects, all it took was to identify and characterize a single function of a simple machine, which leads to the property we care about.

Function or Failure Mode?

Several times over the years we have been called for help on projects where a failure mode had been identified. Perhaps there are leaks on a small percentage of products, leading to the assumption that the leakers are rare. There is a flaw in such logic that often can be seen in door and hatch leaks, and water, air, fuel, and hydraulic leaks, as well as electrical connections and compressed fittings. A small percentage is never the truth. Leaks are evidence of a failed function and always worse than you think. A better way involves just a bit of progressive logic:

- Characterize System Behavior
- Source-Load is the first move
- Identify functions, not failure modes
- Build the E-FAST[2] matrix to diagram the flow of energy through functions.
- Properties dictate the efficiency of functions

---

[2] FAST is an acronym for Functional Analysis Systems Technique. It was developed by Charles W. Bytheway in the 1960s as a Value Engineering tool. We modified and simplified the syntax for our purposes. We put the E in front for Energetic.

One Good Turn

Screws are an inclined plane wrapped around a shaft. Simple enough. The history of screws – different kinds of screws and screwdrivers – is not a short story.[3] Wooden screws might first have been used in wine presses. Metal screws were made one at a time by gunsmiths well into the 1800s.

After discovering that, I spent more than a few hours reading about screws. I decided that I do not have enough years left in this life to do justice to the history of screws and screwdrivers. Such a simple device has so many thread patterns that an Englishman and an American cannot have a discussion on equal footing, given the classifications are so different.

Screws and Boats

I was on my sailboat in the Caribbean and asked the local maintenance guy to change the zincs (sacrificial anodes) – a task for a diver. There are zincs on the end of the prop, rudder support, prop shaft and the bow thruster. The diver was from Spain, the guy in charge from South Africa. There is an Englishman on the next boat over with an accent so thick, I just nodded and agreed with him. I handed the South African boss the zincs and he asked if I had spare stainless steel bolts. I did, and went below and fetched them. He asked if the boat, an Island Packet 445 made in the USA, used that "stupid American measuring system."

I replied, "It's not the American system. The English gave it to us before we threw them out. And the bolts are metric."

The Englishman, who was drinking beer because it was just past noon, jumped in, "At least we had enough sense to get rid of it. You Yanks will never be able to do science with that ancient system." I made a comment about the French having started it with Napoleon, which began a series of

---

[3] One Good Turn: A Natural History of the Screwdriver and the Screw Witold Rybczynski

trading a few more offensive and politically incorrect barbs, but perfectly fine among sailors.

The Spanish diver came up and said one of the bolts he was trying to reuse was bent, and he needed a new one. He handed it to the South African. I looked down from the deck of my boat, and asked, "Is it an M6?"

He gave me a look as if an American couldn't possibly know metric bolt sizes from afar. "It's an M4."

"How long?" I asked.

He replied, "About an inch."

There are screw designs for every application you can think of. Every garage and basement has jars and boxes mixed up with all kinds of screws, but likely not the one you need for the job at hand. If you make a trip to the home improvement store the longest aisle is for screws and nuts, but the nuts are not next to the screws. Good luck! Every junk drawer in every house has at least one screwdriver… but the wrong one or the wrong head for that screw in your hand! The material is not by chance. The material might not matter if you are hanging a mirror on a wall, but it certainly does if you hope to hold a car or an airplane together over many years.

Screws clamp and hold things together by storing potential energy so they don't come apart. When a screw is tightened, it acts as any spring, and strains in proportion to the angular displacement (theta) for a given material and pitch (P). While the screw is stretched (strained) the clamped structure is compressed.

The E-FAST tells the story:

Chapter 1 The Power of a Good Model   19

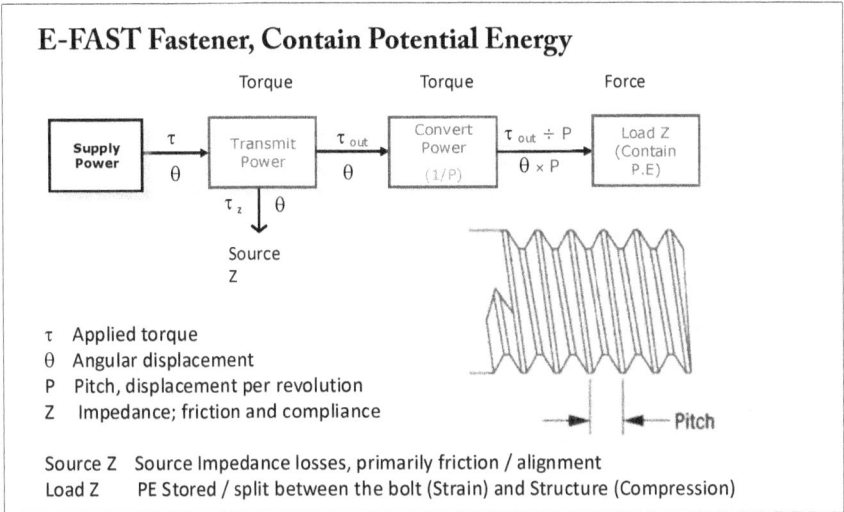

Figure 1-5

Simple enough. But don't take anything for granted. The E-FAST tells the story in a simple way. The model leaves nothing out, but the model is only useful if we use it to see with fresh eyes. The beauty of the model is that it works for tightening screws one at a time by a master toolmaker in his shop, as well as an automatic machine that runs down thousands of screws per day. While the toolmaker can see and feel what is happening, the automatic machine cannot. Screws hold the world together. They are simple multipliers of force, merely wedges wrapped around a shaft. Low-angle wedges are just like the threads on fine-pitch bolts that can create tremendous clamp force when multiplied by a small force applied through a large distance.

There is a copy of *Machinery's Handbook* in my library from 1948. The description of the physics is simple, but the math to tighten a bolt is not quite so. You might put it down thinking, "Wow! There are a lot of ways to, well, screw this up!"

The model shows that to fully characterize the **System Behavior** of creating a clamp load, you need both the torque (effort) and the angular displacement (flow) properly plotted in such a way as to see what is happening.

Figure 1-6 shows that in an effort-based machine, given a constant effort in the vertical axis with varying unseen load such as screw friction, flow can vary dangerously. Controlling effort, such as the torque, is only half the story. We will come to the alternative, a flow-based machine, shortly.

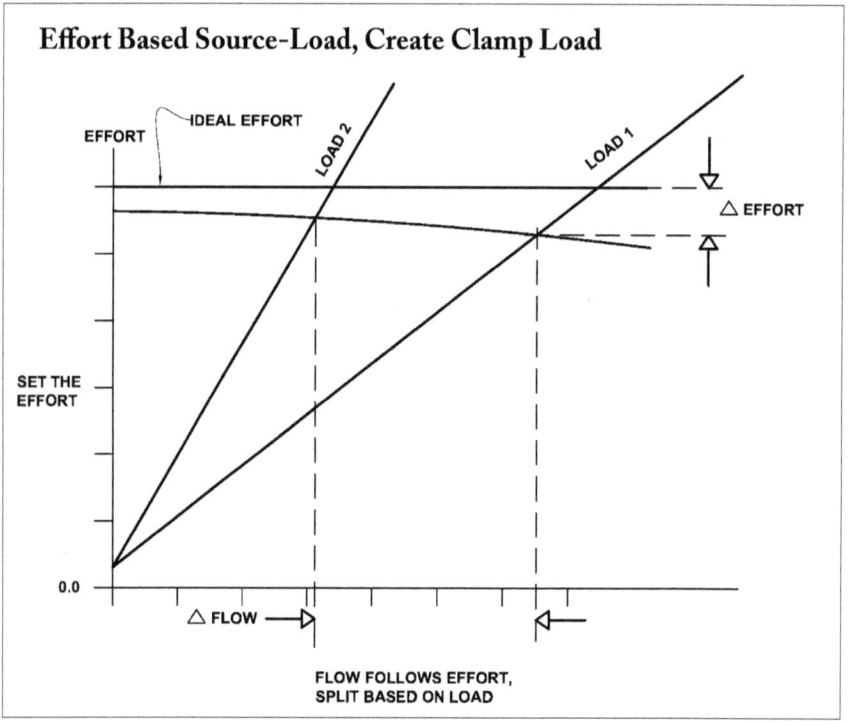

Figure 1-6

There are machines all around the world with air-operated torque drivers, which is like using a spring to push on a spring. Fixed air pressure creates torque while blind to the angular displacement. Quality control might call for a specified torque while claiming the process is statistically capable, but capable of what? Fixed torque means little if the objective is to create a clamp load.

Air-operated tools provide fixed torque (if the air pressure is stable) while angular displacement can vary dangerously. The alternative is electrically operated drivers. Whereas air guns provide fixed torque, electrically operated guns can be easily set to provide fixed displacement. Given that torque is a function of the electrical current to the gun, changes in load are simple to monitor to protect the product.

Characterize System Behavior: Save Lives

There is a long list of projects with some sort of leak over the years. They are simple if you know that a leak is evidence of a failed function. Fixing leaks won't get you far. You have to identify the function. The function, from the 7 × 3 Diagram in Figure 1-4, is to contain potential energy. The property we care about is Compliance, which is a function of clamp load and the structure.

A gasoline tank leaked. It was decided to increase the torque specification for the bolts to a flange. Torque, we now know, is only part of the story. A bolt is a stiff spring, stretched as tightened with a measure of angular displacement. The torque and displacement are conjugates.[4] One cannot be changed without knowing the story of the other... ever! The bolt compresses the mating surface of the tank, which acts like an opposing spring. The compliance of the bolt and the mating surface are balanced and opposite when tightened. That equilibrium must be stable. It wasn't. The tank flange Compliance was such that it quickly released the stored potential energy, which is called creep. Tanks leaked, they caught fire, and lives were lost.

An insulator in an automotive alternator was clamped into place by screws driven by an air-operated torque gun. The torque was fixed but the clamp load varied from too loose to too tight, cracking the insulator. The

---
[4] Conjugates: joined together especially in pairs; acting or operating as if joined

nut friction varied lot-to-lot because of the plating thickness. The angular displacement was as much as 360° greater with slippery nuts, although the torque was constant. Once again, cracked insulators were common but rarely detected by inspection. Flawed alternators were sold and a few caught fire.

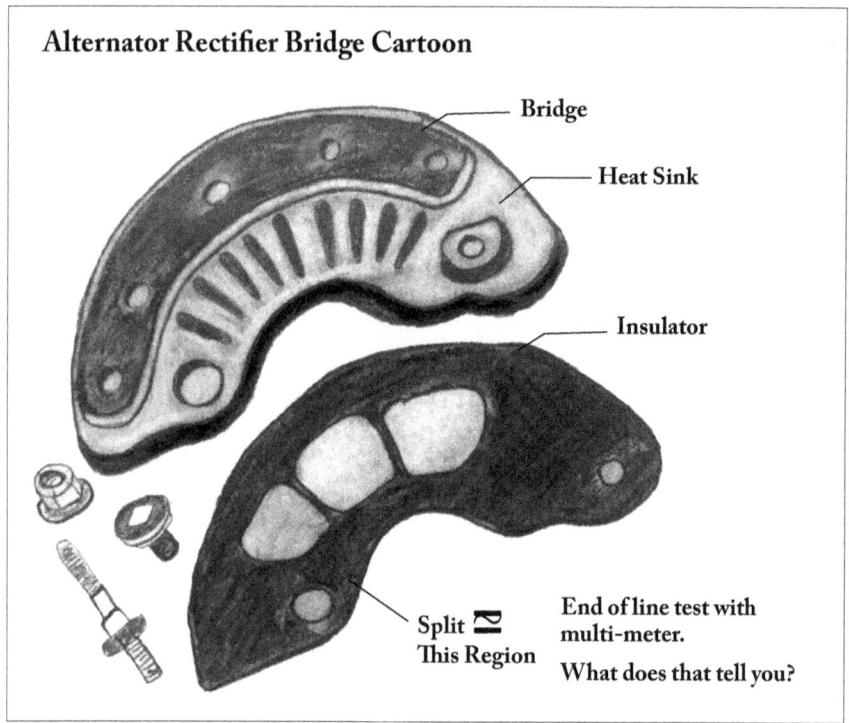

Figure 1-7

Figure 1-7 is a cartoon from my notes. The bolt and nut were the source of the problem. The torque was consistent but the angular displacement, thus the clamp force, varied as the nut friction. Since the clamp force, or the flow, varied, the insulating gasket was subject to cracking.

These are just two examples of terribly expensive problems where smart people were misguided by a flawed strategy of making lists of variables to check. Suppliers all over the world are doing their best to meet the specifications while keeping costs down.

Often, catastrophic events occur because of a nut or a bolt. All it takes is one mistake. The costs to recover can put a supplier at risk. Just meeting the specification is not good enough. Characterize **System Behavior** *based on* **Functional Decomposition** *and sell your products with a lot more confidence.*

Those of us who earn a living making and selling things have a responsibility to our customers to make them safely, to fully understand how they work and the consequences of failure. The story is never just about variables.

The truth lies in **System Behavior**.

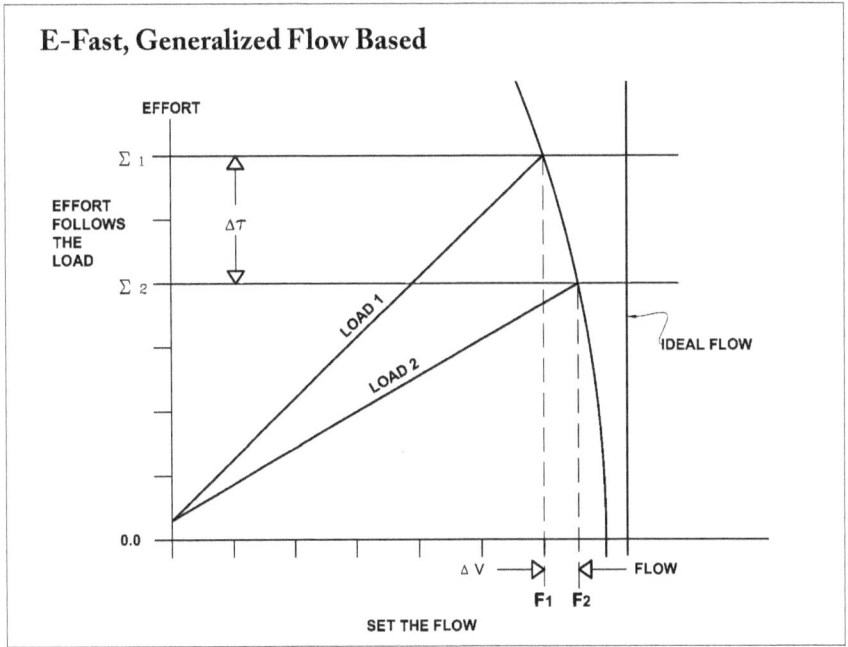

Figure 1-8

Figure 1-8, a general model for flow-based machines, shows what happens with a flow-based machine. If the effort variable on the vertical axis were torque, it would act like a *smart machine*. If the load were to increase because of friction in the screws from Load 2 to Load 1, then the torque, which is proportional to the motor current, would increase, which is shown on the vertical axis. Thus, the torque increases to overcome the load and meet the required displacement, providing proper clamp load.

Figure 1-7, effort-based, shows that a small change in the effort results in a large change in the flow. Figure 1-8, flow-based, shows a large change in the effort results in a small change in flow.

This is an introduction to the importance of the effort-flow workspace and how important it is even in the simple task of tightening a screw!

We have seen how **Source-Load** provides insight into machine behavior where the objective is to supply power, transmit power, and convert power from one domain to another to meet a specific functional objective. The model is powerful and useful for machines we sell, as well as machines we buy and bolt to the floor to make things such as extruders, presses, forges, and so forth – as well as simple assembly machines that tighten bolts. As we have seen, **Source-Load**, properly diagramed with E-FAST, becomes a matrix from supply power through a series of functions to three properties. The linkage is important when the objective is to understand functions, and manage properties. The efficiency of the functions relates directly to properties. If you think the objective is to simply meet a torque specification, you miss the point. The most effective way to see the relationships is to draw them as power and energy flow through machines.

Matryoshka-Small Multiples

We now know there are only two primary strategic approaches needed to characterize **System Behavior**. **Matryoshka-Small Multiples** is the second and often works in conjunction with **Source-Load** to get the full story of what is happening.

Nested Matryoshka dolls are part of Russian culture. The largest outer doll contains a series, perhaps four, of progressively smaller dolls. To see the smaller dolls, you have to open the largest doll, and not fall into the trap of drawing conclusions without looking inside. Historically, **Matryoshka** was used in analogies for nested matrices, such as Markov Processes, creative art, philosophy, psychology, biology, physics, alchemy, and the origins of life. There was a rather interesting movie I saw not long ago where a beautiful woman, a shy young Russian peasant, sold Matryoshka dolls while studying biology in Moscow. She became a model and a dancer, leading to a career as an expert assassin for the KGB and then a double and triple agent. She fell in love, of course, with a CIA agent to add a convoluted level of intrigue. The Matryoshka dolls in the opening of the movie was not lost on me; it was the introduction to the mystery of the story of the woman within the woman.

While **Source-Load** is the story of power, functions, and properties, **Matryoshka** tells the story of functions, processes, and the material beginning with just one cycle. **Matryoshka** is a powerful model to describe the cyclical nature of processes integrated with functions and footprints in a simple matrix. Very often, the output footprint can be characterized – as it also captures the story of the power to process and create the properties of interest. The very nature of characterizing the footprint as imposed by process functions means we need to think of it as a matrix. For maximum insight, we diagram the footprint in increments based on the functions that are imposed by the process in a display dictated by the cyclical nature. This can only be done visually, wearing safety shoes and glasses, with a notebook and a curious eye.

A simple way to explain **Matryoshka** is to use it to tell the story of shape. We have been using machines to create shape for centuries. Today those machines are more sophisticated than ever. **Matryoshka-Small Multiples** helps us see with fresh eyes how to simplify the story within the story of creating shape.

The Limits of Process Capability

The story of shape simply cannot be told with a single feature measured from a collection of parts – often 30 or more across time – then averaged (deviations from the average calculated and limits lines drawn based on probabilistic calculations of what the machine can theoretically do). We then compare the limit lines to specifications, and calculate the risk of out-of-specification dimensions.

If we accept *Process Capability* as a quality control metric, we have to know the limitations. *Process Capability* is a weak diagnostic tool. It loses too much information about machine performance. The name itself is a misnomer. A single measurement of a sophisticated process across multiple parts without regard to machine action tells us little to nothing about the process. It would be more precise to call it a *Parameter Capability*.

That is why we developed **Matryoshka-Small Multiples** – to tell the integrated story of what happens in a single machine cycle while capturing machine action.

Cartooning and Matryoshka-Small Multiples

Cartooning is a process to capture what is happening in a machining or other processing space. Machine tools operate in a three-dimensional space, with a fourth (or more) axis performing within that space. Locating fixtures have a datum scheme to precisely and repeatedly eliminate the freedom of part movement. Cutting tools follow a precise programmed path within the dimensional space. **Cartooning** will capture the path with respect to the datum scheme within that space. It is important to capture the entire story of a cycle. A single measurement of one dimension cannot do the job, made worse by averaging away the story of the machine action.

Cartooning tells the story of how the shape is created. **Small Multiples** *is how we plot the results to see with fresh eyes.* **Matryoshka** *is how we read it and see the story within the story.*

Machining a Cube

Suppose we have to machine a cube from a casting that is part of a larger (theoretical) product of some sort. A few dimensions have been identified as KPCs (key product characteristics). As such, they have been measured across a series of parts, and *Process- Capability* calculated. The KPCs are deemed not capable. The KPCs might be flatness of four sides, parallelism of opposite sides, and perpendicularity of adjacent sides. Each of the KPCs can be described with a single value for each part, calculated from a series of measurements on multiple parts. By themselves KPCs might have value for describing fitness for use. Even so, they can be misleading when averaged and plotted as a distribution. Although a frequent starting point for quality control, there is little diagnostic value with such an approach. We don't just measure dimensions and plot them. It is much more than that. Characterizing **System Behavior** starts with **Cartooning**. **Cartooning** is our process for envisioning, then sketching the integration of the part with tooling structure and datum scheme, as well as the cutters and cutter paths. The cartoon should be a simple sketch or two, not a Rembrandt.

Cartooning Objectives

The objective of **Cartooning** is to describe the part, machining, and machine datum scheme interface. Measurements are taken with respect to the datum-locating scheme and deviations from that scheme. For example, if a surface is programmed to be cut 100 millimeters from an Y-Z plane, the scale on the plot would be set to 0 (zero.) By plotting deviations from the 0 plane, a perfect part would result in a series of points on the zero reference line. Such scaling provides the ability to compare multiple features as deviations, gaining insight into **System Behavior** that cannot be seen any other way.

> *"Data displays must be clear, assured, reliable, sturdy. In designing information, then, the idea is to use just noticeable differences, visual elements that make clear differences, but no more contrasts that are definite, effective and minimal."*
>
> **—Edward R. Tufte**

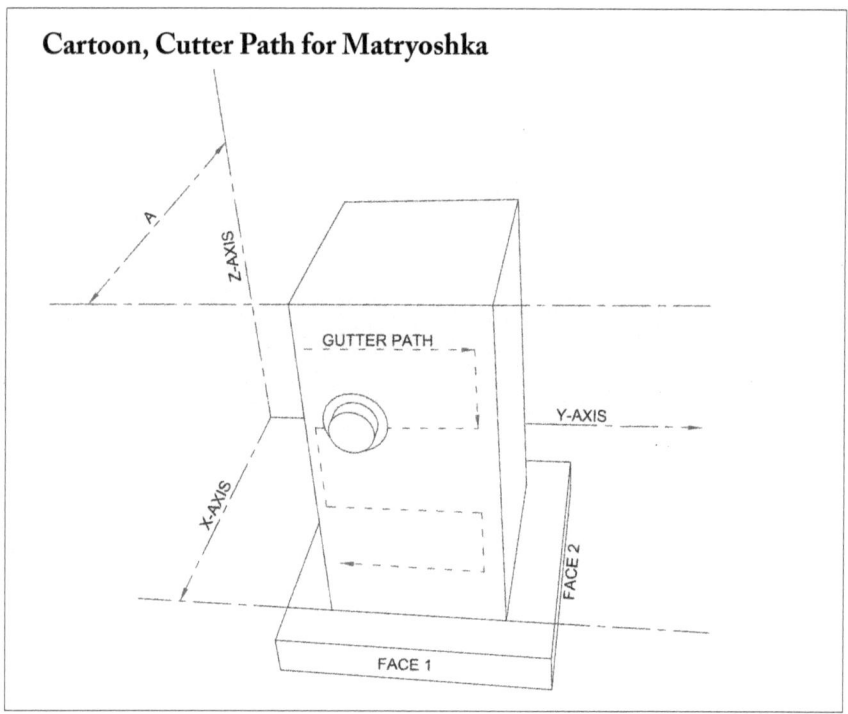

Figure 1-9

Figure 1-9 is a cartoon of a simple cube in a milling machine. The cartoon not only shows the part, but also the part in the machining space and the action of the cutter. The cutter can move in the X, Y, and Z directions while the fixture rotates in the A-axis. The objective of **Cartooning** is to see the machine action, then make the plan to graphically capture the whole story with **Matryoshka-Small Multiples**. A bit of planning is needed once the part is removed from the machine. It is preferable to best replicate the tooling location scheme on the bench in order to really see what is happening. Once located, Face 1 can become the datum reference for measuring that side with respect to the locating scheme. Each touch point has to move a fixed distance in the Y and then Z directions to pick up the cutter path deviations from the Y-Z plane. But what about Face 2? Face 2 has moves in both the X and Z directions, plotting deviations from the X-Z plane. When plotted on **Small Multiples**, each face can be thought of as coplanar, making any deviation from 0 easy to see without any calculations at all.

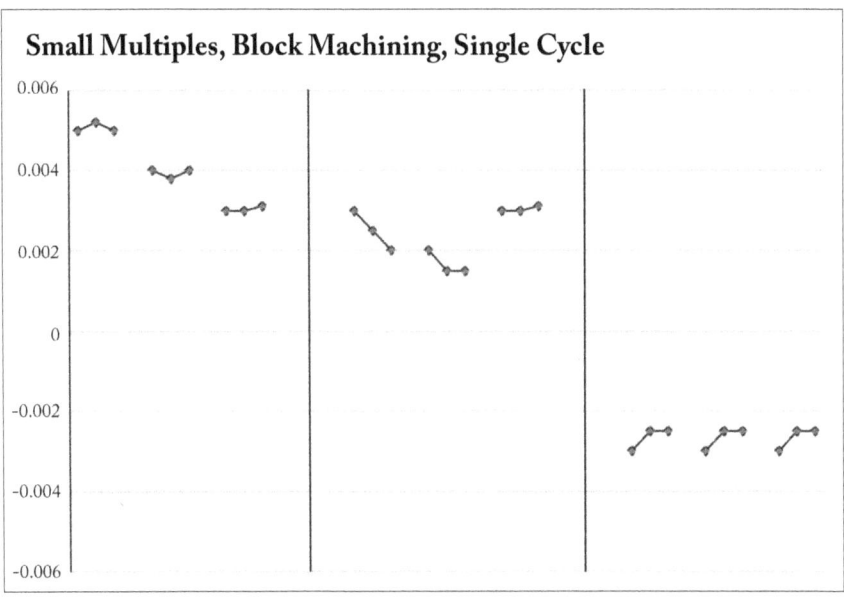

Figure 1-10

| Pass | 1 | 2 | 3 | 1 | 2 | 3 | 1 | 2 | 3 |
| Face | | 1 | | | 2 | | | 3 | |

This is a simple example, but it demonstrates the objectives. Each pass is represented by three measured points. Each pass is separated, as is each face. We can see the smallest effective difference in each pass of the cutting tool then as it moves from face to face as the A-Axis rotates to present each face to the cutter.

Years ago, we had to figure out the complex forming of a large fan blade. Whether or not it was to specification was not the objective, but rather to understand the forming process. The most effective way to see what was happening was to imagine the part as a flat plane and measure deviations from that plane.

The most sophisticated and brilliant application was when David, Tobias, and I were in China. David and Tobias were able to convert the complex geometry of 6-axis machining and grinding a ball screw into a diagram measuring deviations from 0. It was virtually impossible to see the sophisticated machine action of creating a ball screw in any other way. The example led to training the engineers to set up the machines with confidence. With **Matryoshka-Small Multiples** they saw and understood the story within the story.

105mm Howitzer Shells

I was in my office browsing old project notebooks and articles collected and written over the last 30 years. One article that drew my interest was "A Funny Thing Happened on the Way to Inspection" by Robert W. Traver and Cecil A. Blocker, published in 1971, in *Tooling & Production Magazine.*

Bob and his team were working at a company producing 105mm howitzer shells for infantry support, which were manufactured on multiple presses. The client claimed that wall thickness variation was out of spec. As often happens, the inspection system was not suitable for characterizing

System Behavior, which requires measuring with respect to the datum scheme that creates the shape.

Traver describes what he called Variation Research and claims Rath & Strong as the developer. What Traver actually used was a multi-vari created in the 1940s by Len Seder from Gillette Safety Razor in Boston. Len published "Diagnosis with Diagrams" in the early 1950s in *Industrial Quality Control*, emphasizing the importance of the visual power of proper diagrams.

Traver was constrained by the conventional families of variation – within-piece, piece-piece, and time-time – and felt the need to see them all for a complete diagnosis (even though his description of within-piece was flawed). He also fell into the trap of using the measurement system the customer used for quality control, which failed to show the machine action as it creates the part – which is often the case.

At 9 a.m., Traver plotted five single points on each of three machines to represent the variation in wall thickness in 15 parts, then connected them to represent piece-piece. The axis represented within-piece variation – a mistake. Traver used a single value to represent the thickness variation. A single value misses over the machine action, the key to insight and understanding.

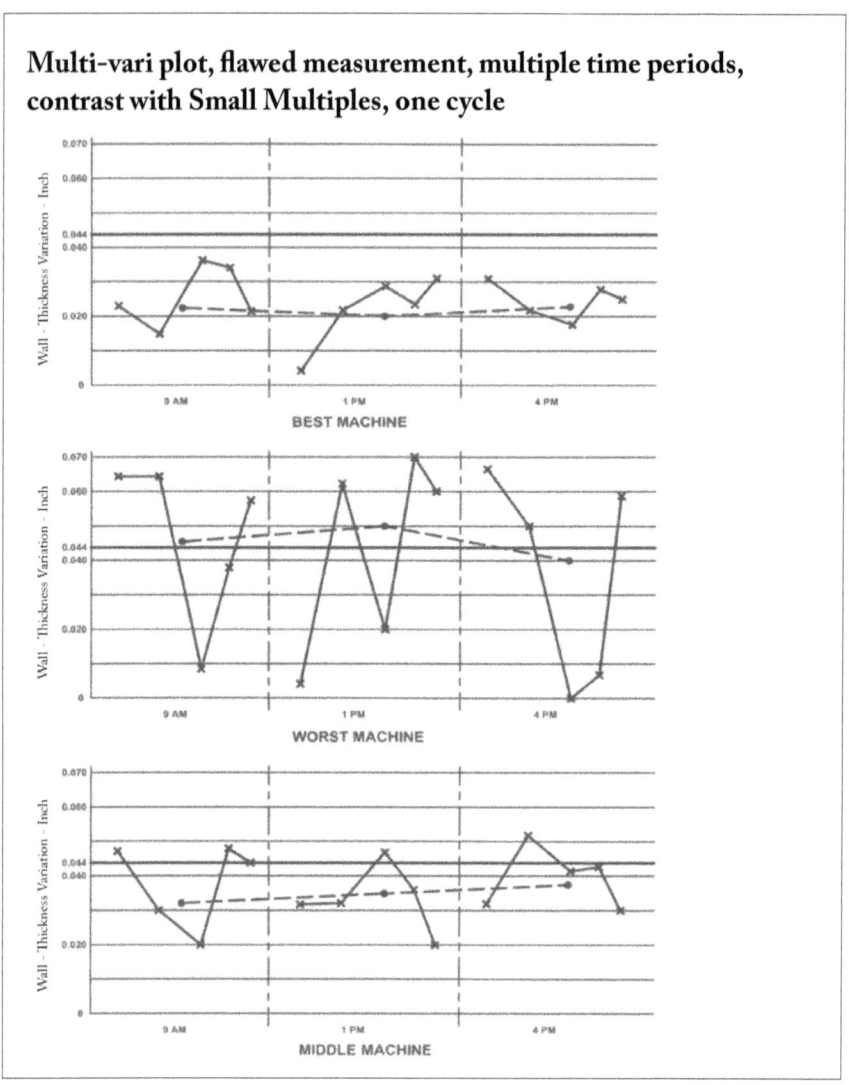

Figure 1-11

There was no indication as to how many locations on the wall were measured, nor the relative position of each with respect to the machine, which is the essence of **Matryoshka** and **Cartooning**. There were clearly multiple readings, likely measured with a micrometer, then the smallest reading subtracted from the largest, reported as wall thickness variation.

This is a common mistake, and we know it as soon as measurements are taken and used for a mathematical operation instead of just plotting precisely what is measured.

What was the shape of the walls? What was the shape of the inside wall with respect to the outside wall? What would the wall look like if we measured the position of the inside and outside wall at, say, 30 degree increments? What do you suppose we might learn if we looked across the part at 180 degrees on three serial parts on just one machine with respect to the press die?

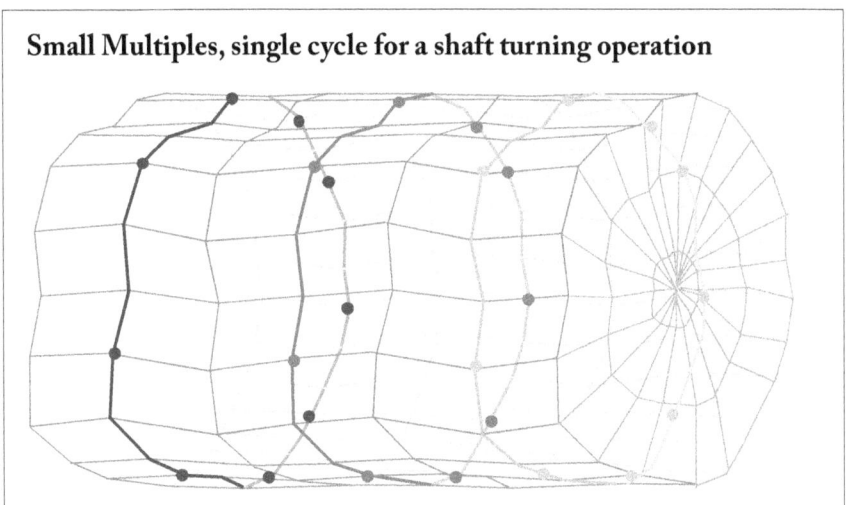

Figure 1-12

Figure 1-12 is the measurement of a cylinder created in a turning operation. Each point is the radial distance from the axis of rotation, the geometric form created by the machine, progressing in the order created by the machine. There are nine radial measurements for each of three progressive circles, defined by the direction of the cutter feed.

Traver measured wall thickness, a calculated value that has nothing at all to do with how the machine operates. **System Behavior** is what we care about. Capture it with **Matryoshka-Small Multiples**. To capture

System Behavior, shape must be measured while capturing orientation with respect to the machine that produced it. This gives you the ability to plot and view shape with respect to the datum scheme of the machine, with the logic of **Matryoshka-Small Multiple** helping to provide a **Causal Explanation**.

Instead of within-part, part-to-part, and time, we capture the elements of sub-cycles, cycles, and super-cycles. This simple change integrates the machine-part interface into the shape measurements and diagram, ensuring visualization of the machine action as the part is created.

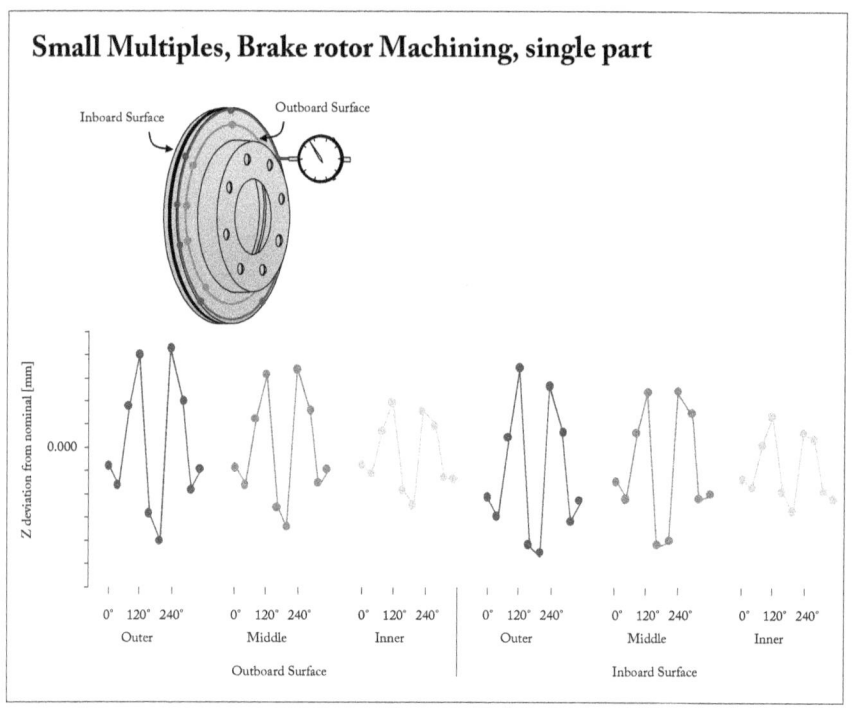

Figure 1-13

Figure 1-13 shows the power of **Matryoshka-Small Multiples** while only measuring a single part in a single machine. There is no need for more if one machine cycle, properly measured, tells the entire story.

The vertical axis is deviation from the nominal. That means, the dial indicator was zeroed against a datumed gauge block, then positioned against the part, retaining position. This is required in order to capture shape, not runout.

The line weight on the rotor matches the **Small Multiple** plot.

The vertical axis is *deviation from the nominal*. That means the dial indicator was not pushed against the rotor, then zeroed, which would only give you runout. The rotor was zeroed on a gauge block, then moved to the part. **Small Multiples** is simple and powerful. It takes a bit of planning and **Cartooning**, which is likely the most important part of the investigation, as the **Small Multiples** plotting intent is to capture the details and action of what you see and draw in the cartoon. The simplicity of what we do is important. Starting with the cartoon, which gives you the chance to really see what is happening, cannot be overstated.

Analysis of variance, t-test, confidence intervals and other statistical techniques, however interesting, are inappropriate because they bury the information contained in the order or production. Such calculations have no application in analytic problems in science and industry.

—**W. Edwards Deming**

Chapter 2

What Is Happening?

I often feel the presence of those who have gone before us. They send me on journeys of discovery as I walk where they did, read what they wrote, experience and see what they made. My mentors are many, but most are from centuries past.

A day or so after the phone rang I was in Hong Kong, waiting for the ferry from Kowloon to Hangzhou. After boarding I looked for the ghosts of Robert Lomax and Suzie Wong. Lomax was a struggling American artist seeking clarity in life in postwar years in a new and confusing culture. They met on this same ferry route in the late 1940s, memorialized in the movie *The World of Suzie Wong*. Suzie Wong, merely a ghost, had lessons as well. Every journey, every person I meet has a story. For every project, for those who learn to see with fresh eyes, it is truly the story within the story where lessons lie.

A driver met me after the ferry arrived on the mainland of China. He carried a sign with my name and spoke no English – but I was used to that before the days of iPhone translation apps. As we drove along the coast of China, I had no idea how long the trip would take, but having grown up on the seacoast of New England, I enjoyed watching people make a living from the sea, seeing new things and different ways of life – good people working hard, many to just survive.

I arrived at the factory that night exhausted. There was a conference call at midnight, with what seemed like a cast of hundreds, as I dropped into a chair fighting to stay awake – made harder by a series of questions that stressed the team but were not helpful. There was a senior executive in the US who had asked me to participate, confident in my ability. Not so the others, whose opinions of me ranged from annoyance to hopeful. I said little, having just arrived.

The next day I was shown around.

There was an apartment building next door where the workers lived that reminded me of a military barracks. The stepper motor is quite small with tiny components. The assembly workers were all girls and young women who worked in a semi-clean room environment, wearing pink lab coats and hats. They were from remote areas of China, grateful for such a job. They worked in shifts to meet the demand. I discovered that each apartment had four beds with eight women assigned to each room. One shift got out of the bed to go to work and the off-shift climbed in. While I was in the submarine service, hot-bunking was common on fast attack boats. The bunk was still warm from the previous sleeper when you climbed in.

The team of too many people wanted to show me all the work they had done. They had done a lot of work, of course, but a lot of work does not necessarily translate into progress.

"The problem is sticking stepper motors. The failure rate is just a few per thousand. Because of the low failure rate, this is a difficult project." That's never true; the failure rate is always much higher. But I said nothing.

"What does it do?" I asked.

"The stepper motor positions a needle for the speedometer, tachometer, fuel gauge, or coolant temperature, and is located in the instrument panel of a vehicle. There can be as many as four in one vehicle. The only ones that stick are the speedometer and tachometer. Once it sticks, if you turn the engine off then restart, it resets, then works. Once we take things apart we cannot find anything wrong. Everything is to spec. We have set up an aggravated screening test in the United States, and find a few that fail. We think we get more failures at elevated temperature and at high motor velocity, meaning it is a higher order interaction. All those that fail are rejected even though nothing can be found wrong. There is little evidence that the screening test has helped reduce field failures, which are expensive. The motor costs $1 but it costs $1,200 to replace it."

"Our team has made a lot of progress, but we still have not found the root cause. We believe this is a higher order interaction."

Little of what I was told was helpful, while much of it was wrong. It hardly mattered as we do not start where others leave off.

There was, of course, a fishbone diagram starting with the four Ms. Let's dispense with these things right away. A fishbone diagram is a model that has absolutely no place whatsoever in engineering technical problem solving, and certainly nothing to do with characterizing **System Behavior**. A waste of time is one thing; but it amplifies wasted time by developing a long list based on useless categories and opinions that someone has to research. The idea is to get a long list, while a professional knows how to keep it short based on a proper progressive search – eliminating where the problem is not – based on taking advantage of how the physical world is organized – and forcing it to reveal its nature.

The quality world has adopted and promoted a set of problem solving tools and have fallen under the illusion that they are universal. They are not. Simple tools may work for simple problems, but simple tools for complex problems can be just plain dangerous. We will show you a proper alternative, develop it, and hopefully change your approach.

In Chapter 1, I made the statement that we solve problems quickly, and that there are constraints we place upon ourselves to keep us on track and focused, based on years of practice. These constraints are part of an effective progressive search strategy.[1] They are so important that I will repeat them over and over. (I actually repeat them over and over to myself on every project!) Once again, I have to remind myself that my role is not to just solve the problem.

This shocks some people, as they think I was brought in to solve a problem. We don't often do that in a day, but when we do it is memorable. We do, however, demand progress toward a **Causal Explanation** each day. That means disciplined **Dynamic Learning**.

If you understand a progressive search and the importance of effective questions, then learning one thing at a time is just logical. How to frame the questions in a proper progressive search takes a bit of skill and practice. We want to help you get that practice.

Quite often, the way a problem is defined includes flawed statements and conclusions. We are always on the lookout for this, especially when a team is working furiously and getting nowhere.

The problem was defined as a stuck indicator. Once I looked at what they were doing, it was clear they thought it was mechanical impedance, which includes friction. That might have been the case, but there are other possibilities. A proper progressive search must begin with a question that includes everything. It must also be phrased in such a way so that given knowledge of how a machine or process is physically organized, you can eliminate where the problem is not. Processes and machines are physically organized in natural groups. A proper progressive search provides the opportunity, by testing, to eliminate groups, not single variables. It takes care and a bit of practice to learn; but this is important.

The team was taking actions and making changes based on fishbone diagram variables, which included having the workers change garments more often, replacing the normal air filters to expensive HEPA (high

---

[1] Progressive Search is a process of elimination based on forcing a product or process to reveal its nature. Identifying the natural divisions of a process or product is the first tactical move. English poet laureate John Dryden, 1631-1700, said, "Happy the man who, studying Nature's Laws, through known Effects can trace the secret Cause."

efficiency particulate air filters), and adding an oiling operation to a bowl feeder for a pinion that was the size of a grain of rice. Each action was a possible answer to the question "What's wrong?" – to no avail. The only response they had was the percentage of field failures. Relying on percentages and parts per million is a great way to get fooled. This never works as a problem solving response. The physics of failure, if present in any part, are discoverable. Learning how will give you the opportunity to become an extraordinary problem solver.

We always need an effective strategic question, which is far more simple and powerful than a problem definition. Such a progressive search question:

- Includes every possibility. Yes, all of them!
- Has leverage, in that an answer eliminates where the problem is not.
- Provides new knowledge.
- Is strategically sound, meaning we get an answer fast. In order to be strategically sound, it must have a level of simplicity.
- Each answer leads to the next question.

The only way this works is if the Question is based on Functional Decomposition, or simply "What's happening?" – not "What's wrong?"

As I said earlier, defining the problem as a stuck indicator is a conclusion that might be flawed, but that does not mean it is not possible – but rather, hidden in the response, which is a percentage, or parts per million, of failures.

At the time, I knew little about the operation of stepper motors. I have been fooling around with electromagnets and coils since I was a boy. I built a DC motor for a science project when I was 12. I knew that rotors chased after an inductive field and the current is a function of the torque load.

Actually, that's not quite true. I learned that like-magnetic poles (N-N, S-S) repelled, and opposites attracted. I learned that with brushes, which are clever switching devices, the polarity would reverse and the rotor would rotate. (Big deal? Well, for me it was. There was no YouTube so I had to go to the library on my bike.)

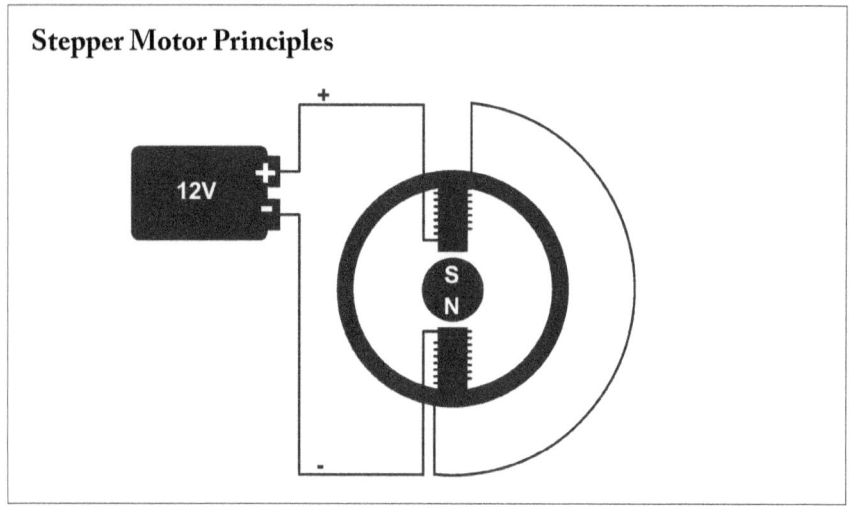

Figure 2-1

If we built such a device as the one above, the rotor would remain stationary and magnetically locked. That is how a stepper motor would behave if, for example, a vehicle was traveling at constant speed with the cruise control set. The coils are energized and the magnetic rotor aligns with the field.

If the battery leads are reversed, the rotor would rotate 180 degrees and once again remain magnetically locked. Let's add another set of coils and a series of gears for more precision, remove the battery, and replace it with a microprocessor that follows the table below, where zero means no voltage. If the processor sequences down the table, the rotor will rotate 360 degrees. The displacement of the pointer depends on the gear ratio. Now the processor can position the pointer up or down in small increments, fast or slow to reflect engine RPM, vehicle speed, or even the level in the fuel tank. We can step on the gas or slam on the brakes and the indicator will move rapidly.

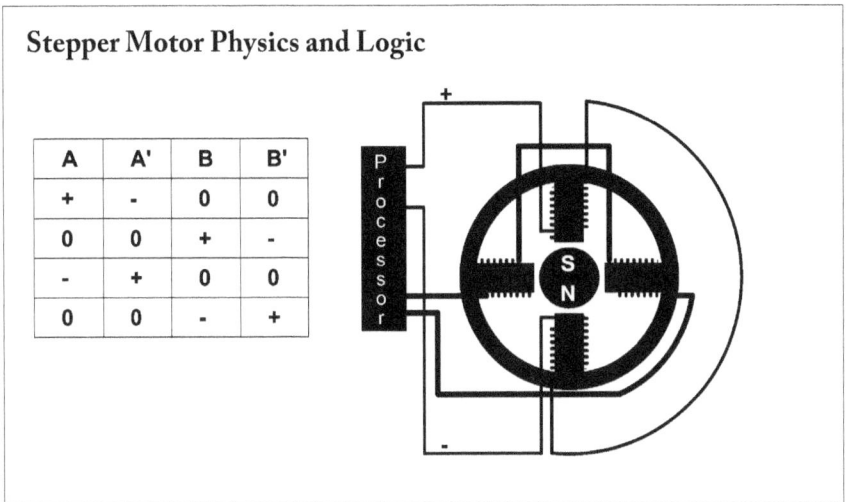

Figure 2-2

For the speedometer, the principal input comes from a sensor on the wheel. Remember that the team told us that the problem manifested itself at high velocity. High velocity does not mean the vehicle is going 100 miles per hour (160 kph). If the cruise control were set at that speed the stepper motor would be stationary and magnetically locked, making minor adjustments.

Let's assume the driver is going fast, sees a police car, then slams on the brakes and locks the wheels. Now the stepper motor has to position the indicator as fast as it can to the zero position from near the upper limit of the face.

Since the switching device is driving the rotor as fast as it can, I suspected that it was not really getting mechanically stuck. Things don't generally get stuck at high speeds then free themselves when all you do is turn the system off and back on. If a rotor gets stuck at high speed, in my recollection, they generally stay stuck or leave a bit of evidence if they don't.

Let's get away from the simple concept diagram and look at something more realistic.

The stator is quite fascinating, in that it is just a fine-blanked plate with a shape to direct the flux that positions and increments the magnetic rotor. The positioning logic follows the table in Figure 2-3 except that the actual stepper motor has three stator positions so the rotor increments are 120 degrees, not 90 degrees. It is worth mentioning that the origin of this motor is in the watch industry. An even smaller one would fit in your grandfather's watch.

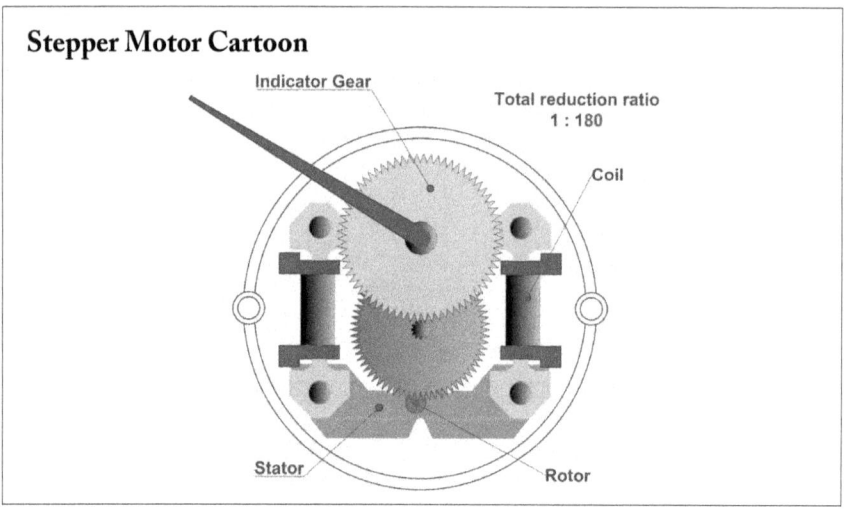

Figure 2-3

Now we have an idea as to how this works – but I still haven't formulated a strategic question.

What's Happening?

Once again, the first question has to include everything while providing the leverage to execute. In other words, a question has no value if we cannot get an answer quickly and decisively and it progressively leads to the next question.

I suppose there is a point to make here. We have worked all over the world on problems where others were frustrated. Often people are brilliant but their strategy is flawed. They are usually fun to work with. A few might suffer from the Dunning-Kruger effect. I was introduced to this by a friend who is a cardiologist. "Many young doctors," he said, "are brilliant but have little experience, have high confidence and low knowledge, and can be quite difficult to convince of another way to look at something." I suggest their models are flawed. Everyone, given a chance, wants to learn a better way.

Many years ago, David and I went to a tire plant in Canada. I will never forget because it was -23 degrees Fahrenheit. We were in Canada so it was actually -30 degrees Centigrade. The plant manager had invited us – and called the quality manger to take us on a tour, telling him we were there to help solve the toughest and most chronic problems. He asked, "How long have you guys been in the rubber business?"

"About 15 minutes," replied David. The quality manager rushed us through the tour.

By noon that day, we had a **Causal Explanation** for a costly chronic problem. They were not looking at it in an effective way. Their model was flawed. What did we do? We know how the physical world is organized and how to take advantage of it. We might have been in the rubber business for 15 minutes, but there is nothing you can do with machines in a tire plant that we have not seen before in fascinating applications by brilliant scientists, engineers, and other experts.

One Good Question!

We don't need to know how every machine works; but we do need to know the fundamentals of machine behavior and how to take advantage of it. As we always do, we need to get that first question formulated. *All this project needed was one good question and the rest fell into place.* They were working with a long list. The project, as many do, fit neatly into just two categories. The entire list could be split into two: input or function[2]. A simple test was all it took to learn one important thing. I cannot recall ever learning from a list. Maybe it is because a list is the absence of any form of learning, and violates the constraint of *learning one thing every day*. If you are in a leadership role, your strategic job is to make sure teams are effectively learning. Learning is staying on track. It is also fun.

Learning Is Everything!

The stepper motor might have been a bit more complicated than the project in the tire plant; but once again, we know our job was not to solve the problem – but rather to learn one thing about the physics of function and failed function in a progressive search for a **Causal Explanation**. I try to be careful about people labeling me a problem solver. It is what we do; but problem solvers have been labeled as the folks with the bag of tools.

We prefer to think of ourselves as Dynamic Learners... fast, clever, and effective, constrained by models and principles.

A young design engineer from Switzerland was assigned to help me with the stepper motor, as I could find no one at the manufacturing company that knew enough about how the motor really worked to get to the bottom of this. I really needed his help. My first inclination, before I made the sketches above, was to think of monitoring the current with respect to

---

[2] Isolation is one of only four strategies, described fully in the companion book, Diagnosing Performance and Reliability, by David Hartshorne.

angular velocity and displacement. Well, they were motors! "You have the wrong model in your head," the young engineer said. Off to the whiteboard we went!

After an hour or two, I said, "Is it true that the problem we are seeing fits into one of these two buckets of physics?" I had made a sketch on the whiteboard as follows:

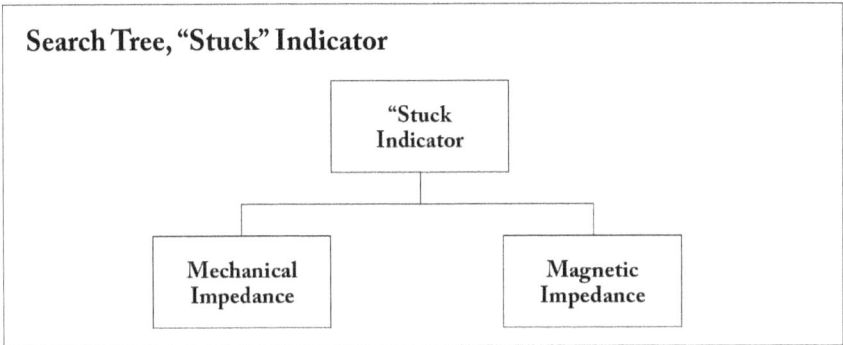

Figure 2-4

It is times like this that I wish David was around. I like our discussions of whether or not the first question will really do what we want. Many people around the world have said how much they like to watch these discussions as well as the evolution on the whiteboard as David, Tobias, and I trade the pen and eraser. These are wonderful examples of **Dynamic Learning**. The Swiss engineer was concerned that if there was an electrical problem it might not be included. I replied that if there were an electrical problem, even if caused by the logic, it would manifest itself as magnetic impedance. I then said, "I know I can measure the electrical properties like volts and amps, but it won't do any good. If I cannot measure magnetic impedance, then splitting the stepper motor into the two buckets of physics, even if true, is useless."

"I can measure it," he said. "But the failure rate is in parts per thousand. We might have to measure a lot of them."

"Not so! There are always a lot more of them than you think. Let's get to it!" Within a day we had a test set up on the manufacturing line hooked up to the final test station. Now we could see how well the stepper motors worked, not *if* they worked.

Figure 2-5 shows interesting results. What does it mean? The coils are powered with volts and the current is a function of the load to create a magnetic field. The polarity is plus, minus, or neutral in order to manage the direction of the rotor. This sounds simple enough, until you try to do it 1,000 times per second when, for example, you are going 160 kph and step on the brakes. Now the precision and timing matters. The coil does not come on and off like a lightbulb. Think in terms of a flywheel that starts from a dead stop, has to wind up to perform useful work, then comes to a complete stop, then winds up in the opposite direction. If this has to happen rapidly, then the flywheel stops and starts like a bicycle wheel where a stick is jammed into the spokes!

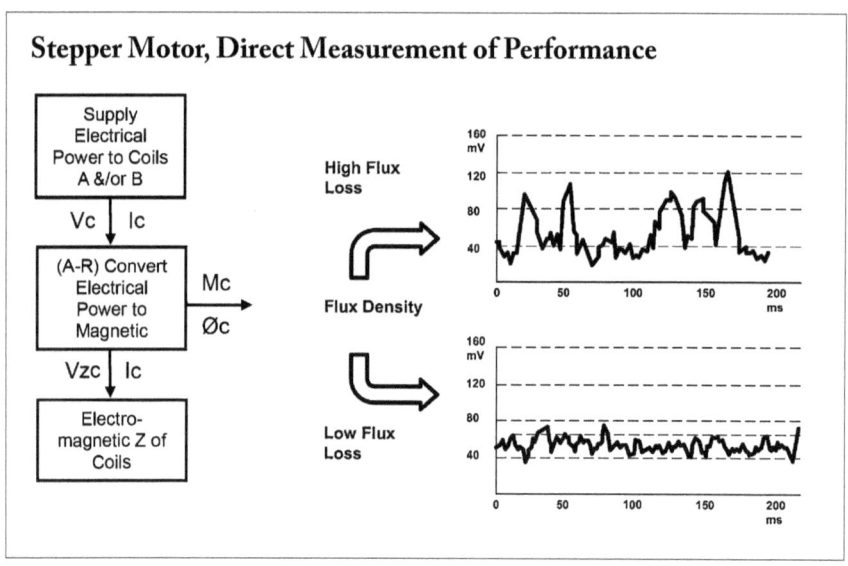

Figure 2-5

What we are looking at in Figure 2-6 is a properly calculated measurement of the back electromotive force (EMF), or the counter EMF, which opposes the magnetic force to rotate the rotor. It is easy to see in the ugly stepper motor. Back EMF is a phenomenon that is always present. For some reason, in the ugly stepper motor, it is higher than expected, thus the effort left to spin the rotor is low.

Why? The counter, or back EMF, is created when the axis of rotation of the tiny magnet molded into the plastic rotor is not centered in the fine-blanked stator hole. No, I did not know this right away and I would not expect you to either. But Figure 2-6 provided the means to ask. In Figure 2-6 you can see that the rotor is so far off center that it hits the side of the hole. Now look at the rotor below David's finger and you can get a feel for the size!

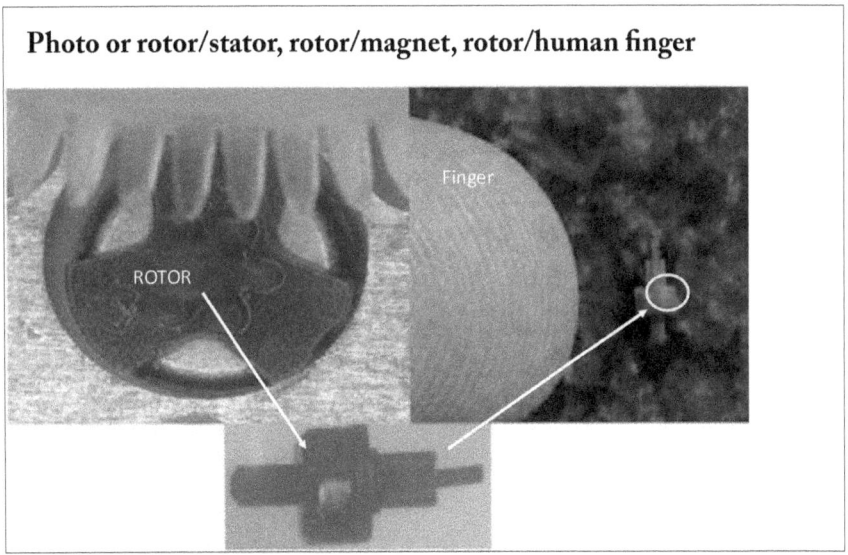

Figure 2-6

We are getting close to a **Causal Explanation**! When the rotor is not straight, the back, or counter EMF, is high and the torque available to rotate the rotor is low. If the torque is low, and the rotor actually touches the side of the hole, the logic loses its place and stops. In other words, the logic has to know where the rotor is in order to tell it where to go. If position is lost, the next step cannot be directed, so the motor just gives up. The logic resets when the car is turned off then on. That is not a stuck rotor, but rather a step loss. And it is beginning to make sense why it happens only at rapid motor speed, what with all the rapid energizing, de-energizing, and reversal of the coils.

We have learned a lot, but still do not quite have a complete **Causal Explanation**.

Why Are the Rotors Not Straight?

It only took a short time to collect a few ugly rotors. Even being so tiny, there was a mold and cavity number on them, which quite surprised me, although you needed a microscope to see it. The ugly rotors all came from the same few cavities on the mold and were the most remote, or furthest from the injection point. Being the furthest, they would see the lowest injection pressure. When making precision plastic parts, there is always a rapid-fill cycle, then a slow, high-pressure cycle called packing, then a hold cycle to maintain the pressure while the part takes on its shape. What you are doing is jamming strain energy into the parts to preserve shape, a bit like making tempered glass. The idea is to keep it there through its life. When it is released, it is called creep. We knew the most remote parts were the ones that had failed, but the parts that we looked at that were new looked okay. I don't remember how many parts were from each shot (cycle) but let's say it was eight or so. We had to sort through the box from the supplier to get rotors from each cavity as they were all mixed. I wanted to help, but I was too slow and elbowed out of the way. Maybe it was three from each cavity, or 24 parts or so. It would have been far simpler if we could have selected parts by cycle before the sprue was removed, but the mold was in Eastern Europe and we were in China.

We put them all in an oven after a discussion about how hot and how long. I know we discussed the temperature the stepper motor would see by leaving a car in the sun in the desert for a while, which made sense. We didn't want to melt them, but rather see if the rotors that were most remote in the mold yielded and bowed first.

After enough time for a long coffee break, we took them out and looked at them under the microscope. The ones that lost their shape were all from the remote cavities with varying degrees of loss of straightness. No one was interested in sorting the rotors by cavity in the boxes of parts, so the remote cavities were blocked in the die and the parts we had were scrapped. Now we were close to confidently being able to make and sell a functioning product with confidence, but we had to make sure we proved to ourselves we knew the full story.

The motor had not been in production for long – likely less than a year. The stator hole where the rotor rotated was, interestingly enough, currently close to the minimum spec. The size distribution was quite small, meaning the precision of the fine blanking operation was extraordinary. As the die wears, the hole gets smaller, which makes sense. It had been a year. A smaller hole made it easier for the rotor that was not straight to hide the side.

Once we got this far, the team leader from quality suggested increasing the specification for the hole size in the stator so a sloppy rotor had clearance. It might make sense on one level, but we need to have the entire story and understand physical interdependencies before considering such changes. This suggestion did get me to think about the hole size and measure it under a microscope.

The EMF available to turn the rotor depends on the stator-rotor geometric relationship. Not only would making the hole bigger decrease the EMF to power the rotor, but the rotor, not being straight, would still have a counter EMF. If the hole were beyond a certain size, it would actually make the problem worse because the flux density would decrease, thus less power to turn the rotor.

The team wanted to follow the existing procedure for validation testing to confirm the **Causal Explanation**, but I was wary. How did they pass validation in the first place? Why should we have faith in a test that allowed this and the associated staggering costs to occur?

Remember, the stepper motor had been approved for production less than a year prior. I was curious about the validation testing. I am always curious about validation testing because there is often a strategic flaw in the testing because the objective is just to pass!

How Well Does It Work?

The stepper motors had passed, of course. There was some number of hours a sample of motors had to run without failing an abusive test, which related to vehicle life. *As often happens, the idea is to survive the test. The weakness of such testing is that it might be the wrong question.*

Suppose we ask, "How well does the motor work when we first put it to the test, and how well does it work at certain test intervals, including the end of the test?" That is a powerful question that merits further discussion. Don't just break things! Measure the functional performance before they break!

Chapter 2 teaches us to apply the **Source-Load** model to gain new knowledge about performance. We had the performance test we needed as demonstrated earlier by measuring back EMF with the modified end of line test. Back EMF is power loss, which the **Source-Load** model told us to characterize.

"You guys still have the old motors you used for validation testing?"

"I think so!"

A technician rummaged through his desk drawers and claimed victory. "I found them!" We measured these old motors on our new test rig. Some looked fine, but some were worse than anything we had measured so far.

The fine blanked rotor holes in the stator were close to the upper spec limit, as they were made when the die was new. They worked, but poorly. They had limped across the finish line like a gasping marathon runner.

The ability to figure this out in a simple way is important. Once we stopped trying to figure out what was wrong, and changed the question to find out what was happening in a search for a **Causal Explanation**, we had a chance.

The physics are there to see… you have to be clever enough to find a way. It's your job! And it's fun! It is why I keep doing it at an age when most people are retired.

Parts per thousand is a quality metric, not a performance indicator.

If there were one message I would have, it is that you are deluding yourself if you are trapped thinking parts per thousand or even parts per million is a performance indicator. It is always worse! Much worse!

Avoid running diagnostic tests such as swapping parts around without first finding a parameter that helps you see the physical world and execute a proper search.

Perhaps the team on the stepper motor could have swapped rotors around, but so what if the response was a stuck rotor after hours of testing? Who cares? The back EMF was the key! The back EMF was high in about 25 percent of the manufactured parts! The fault manifested itself once the rotor bore got close to the lower spec limit. Back EMF was visible with proper testing. It took forever to find a *stuck rotor*.

In over 30 years and hundreds if not thousands of projects, neither David, Tobias, nor I can recall a single project where a failure rate measured in percentage was a proper representation of the flawed physics. The problem is always worse than you think… much worse.

*In the mind of a scientist, beauty is simplicity.
The most elegant experiment is one that takes no time
to set up and gives the answer to every question.*

—**Weike Wang**

Chapter 3

Models and Simplicity

The importance of a deep and rich understanding of models is key to being an effective learner and problem solver. It is also important to living a good life.

Most of the readers will be aware of the George Box[1] quote, "All models are wrong. Some are useful." Thanks, George. Now what? Where does that leave us? How do we know if a model is useful since only some are?

What is a model? Is a model ever the truth? How do I know if a model is completely wrong? How much time is needed to figure it out? If a model really is wrong, given our nature, will we be willing to let it go? History tells the story of the unwillingness of so many to see the simplicity of a new way of doing much of anything, that we hold onto old models tightly, even as we profess to be agents of change.

Letting Go of Old Models

Models are how we see and approach the world, and how we react to it. Models help us sort out what matters in a structured way. Models help us to organize and divide complexity into logical groups. If you read the

---

[1] George Box was a British statistician and son-in-law of the famous Sir Ronald Fisher, who was credited with developing designed experiments while working in agricultural research.

history of science, great discoveries are made by brilliant people capable of model-based thinking. Be wary of models that are dogmatic in nature. Be flexible, ready to adjust whenever the evidence merits.

> *Alexander Hamilton [founder of the US Banking system] had tried to explain the concepts he had learned in Malachy Postelthwayt's Dictionary of Commerce. But as often happened, stubborn assumptions impeded comprehension. In Alexander's experience, prejudice and ignorance were the brick and mortar of men's prisons. Say "bank" and otherwise sane gentlemen foamed at the mouth and started barking. He knew with scientific certainty what would save the revolution from economic collapse, but he might as well teach Greek to the Cochran's Scottish terrier.*
>
> —*The Hamilton Affair: A Novel* by Elizabeth Cobbs

Models are not just how we solve technical problems, but also how we see and interact with the world and people around us. My first job out of college in the US Navy was at a small factory 15 minutes from my house. There was no travel to suppliers, or anywhere for that matter. Almost everyone had the same cultural background and likely voted for the same candidates. Everyone looked like me. We just did our jobs and went home. Few people work like that anymore, and I think that's a good thing. It was stifling! Not only do we need to question models for solving problems, but also for how we see the world around us. They go hand-in-hand, and that makes life fun and interesting.

Keep It Simple

Several years ago, I had a project at a US automobile company in the powertrain division. The president of the division, whom I greatly admired, had shut down the line because of a problem, starving the assembly plant for a new vehicle model. It did not take long to figure out the problem, but there were sure a lot of people watching! At the review with what seemed like a packed house, one hourly guy said with a bit of frustration, "I don't know why we had to bring him in here," meaning me. "Everything he said was just common sense." I didn't quite know how to take his comment so I approached him. What frustrated him was the massive and confusing structure built around the problem-solving teams – so much that progress was difficult if not impossible – a structure that defied the logic of models and simplicity. Almost every so-called action item meant one more task for him, always to no avail. The fact is that he had common sense, and plenty of it. The nature of the physical world is simplicity. He knew it, but could not quite express it. Our job is to help people just like him learn. Sometimes the structure is in the way.

Da Vinci said, "Simplicity is the ultimate sophistication." Simplicity has to be guided and constrained by models leading to learning and gaining insight into **System Behavior**. Models that guide you to gain insight into **System Behavior** are as close to the truth as possible. You will not see the simplicity of the physical world if you are wandering around collecting data without a sound approach based on effective questions guided by the nature of things. In the kind foreword that David wrote, he said we collect observations and turn them into information. What he wrote means that we do not collect lots of data then analyze it. It is observations we seek! Learning to observe and to turn observations into information will help you become an extraordinary problem solver.

David and I were recently talking about the importance of effective models and the work we have done for many years, striving for effective learning. "Everything becomes simple if you have the right model," he said. If you are struggling, perhaps a flawed model is a barrier.

I sometimes wonder if human nature finds complexity where it isn't, or perhaps if complexity is merely the absence of an effective model. I suppose I could also say that the absence of an effective model clearly stated is useless. Without an effective model you are doomed to wander aimlessly.

> *Things always begin by being complicated, but when we put the effort in to understand them, they become simpler.*
>
> **—Francois Michelin**

Models are supposed to help simplify complexity. Flawed models will do the opposite, especially if applied dogmatically with no regard to any other way of thinking.

What we have done is put together a thinking frame, a **Dynamic Learning** map applying models that work together to encourage understanding and dialogue while effective constraints keep us on track. The XO Learning Map effectively integrates **First Principles** with **Expert Knowledge**, which we have learned is the only way to innovation.

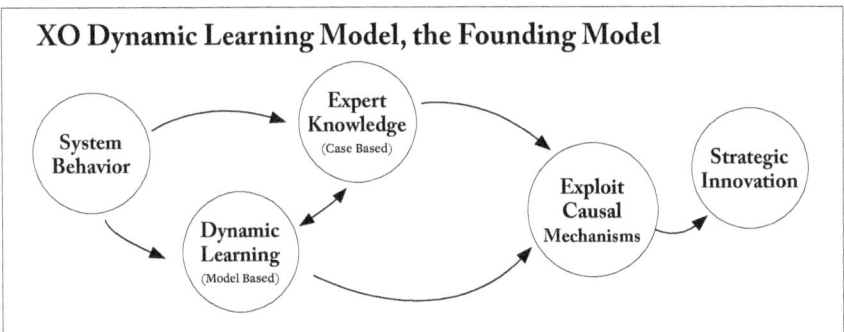

Figure 3-1

Without such a framework, simplification only works to a point, followed by failure. Simplification can be limited by labels and universal application of rules and standardization, which impedes innovation. The goal of simplification is fitness for the application intended. Shoehorning the world into a single model reeks of dogma, impeding creativity and, most importantly, innovation.

With every single project, the objective is to find the ultimate simplicity that will reveal itself if sought while constrained by principles, proper models, and meaningful questions, executed in a thinking frame or Learning Map. That is the essence of strategic excellence. We have to see the world of problematic machine behavior as coherent, being held together by a set of principles. And machine behavior is held together by governing principles! Unnecessary complexity, dogma, and claims of intellectual ownership threatens coherence. Models that fly in the face of governing principles, such as fishbone diagrams that have no basis in science, should never be used to help solve product performance problems.

"Everything should be made as simple as possible, but no simpler" is a quote that can be attributed to several people. Few people seem to get it just right. Models are compressions, and when presented as such, they are effective and as close to the truth as possible. A Search Tree is an effective model for gaining insight into functional decomposition based on **System**

Behavior, and it poses statements of alternatives, one of which must be a representation of the truth. Common or special causes are not realistic alternatives. They provide no clear boundaries defined by physical principles, just the dogma of probability as a poor substitute for the physical world or **First Principles** and truth.

Awareness and an open mind lead the way to changing how we see the world around us in every domain, even how we see life. Sometimes it takes a life-changing event, such as waking from a month-long coma and being told, "John, you need a heart transplant." That got my attention! It was a life-changing moment if there ever was one.

Anode Coating

Four months after receiving the Gift of Life, my new heart and I were in a hotel in Hangzhou, China, which was 1.5 kilometers from the factory. I walked every day. Across the street from the hotel there was a park where I could take a break if I left early enough. Every morning, a woman led a tai chi group of maybe ten people dressed in proper colorful costumes. My heart was new and my gratitude for life was rich and growing. Each day became a gift and I was learning to take pleasure in that gift. It is wonderful how beautiful life really is around this amazing world once you have been so close to death. The interesting thing is that I learned to take the work I was doing less seriously, and found I was more effective.

The company in China made lithium batteries for the auto market. I was there for one project, which is described in Chapter 8, but had some free time while waiting for this or that, and asked for another project to fill the time. The quality manager asked me to have a look at the *Process Capability* of one of the coating lines for the anode. The anode is made from a carbon and graphite mixture coated onto a copper foil, current collector. The copper is a foil strip thousands of meters long, unrolled as it is coated, and rolled up again at the end of the line. It then went to calendaring (squeezed between large rolls) and later cut to size.

The quality manager handed me a thumb drive with 18 months of coating weight data. I made the mistake of trying to open the file that was so big it locked my computer. *Process Capability* was calculated in periodic intervals that had no practical value. They had fallen into the trap of collecting gigabytes of data based on flawed models. The mental model was so rigidly embedded into their thinking that they assumed the answer was in the data. Perhaps they were a data driven company! Many times we are asked for help by leadership, then have to politely sit through a presentation of data analysis that has nary a clue as to the truth of what is happening. The model of *we are a data driven company* has driven many to collect mountains of data that contains little information. Instead of data, we need to collect observations based on first posing a question that, once answered, will turn observations into information. It takes but a few observations if the question is sound. Data collection and analysis has become too easy and too big, and ultimately expensive when done remotely. Observations are dynamic and active. Data collection is passive.

> *About 25 years ago, David and I were teaching a seminar for the quality department of a new client. We were just starting out on our own, confident but wary. After all, nothing happens until something is sold and every new project is important. David was describing the ideas and concepts we were developing, which were in their infancy. One person raised his hand and said, "My job is to take data that someone else collects and do the analysis. If I were to do what you propose, I will have to learn how machines really work." He had no intention of doing so. We were both crushed, and we wondered if we would still be in business in a month, never mind 25 years.*

Once freed from the prison of data, we needed to observe the dynamics of how the process worked. Coating weight is measured by punching a precision square from the coated web and weighing the value of the copper and the coating on both sides. Next, one side is stripped and weighed again. The other side is stripped and is weighed once more. When weighed again you have the weight of the coating removed from each side, and can simply calculate the mass per unit of area you choose as long as you recognize that the larger the area the more risky the calculation. In battery production, uniformity really does matter. Lack of uniformity increases the risk of hot spots as well as a couple of other problems where the consequences are severe.

My new Chinese team member and I walked to the coating line. I started to make a couple of sketches – no photographs. A sketch is a way to commune with the system – the beginning of understanding. Da Vinci said that you draw what you see. You might say those who cannot draw cannot see. Seeing **System Behavior** is beyond just problem solving. It is part of the **Dynamic Learning** process, and it's supposed to be fun. A sketch is the key to opening the Black Box hidden in data. A cartoon is key to identifying functions and to learn how they perform together to create a product or another function. A sketch can be a challenge because it forces you to understand machine functions and interrelationships of functions. The sketch lets you see – to learn what and when to measure in order to characterize the functions quickly. How functions work together gives you the ability to quickly understand **System Behavior**.

Broken Reamers

Years ago, we were asked to help in an engine plant where reamers were snapping off in bored holes for valve guides. Once again, we were told it would be difficult as it rarely happened. We all now know the model of *rarely happened* is flawed. The physics were always there; a broken reamer was an extreme manifestation of the physics.

I was taken with what they thought was to be a quick tour of the line. The engine heads were located on a series of fixtures. The fixtures were on a transfer line, which means the fixtures moved from station to station for each operation. We are often escorted on a quick tour of a line and then expected to head back to the conference room to talk about it.

"Can you get me a chair and leave me here for a bit?" Two chairs were brought out so one person could stay with me as I made sketches and notes. The sketches were limited to the drilling operation, which was done at one station, then the reaming operation took place at the next station. Any error in location of the drilled hole in the first operation stressed the reamer in the following operation as it entered the hole. Once we had an idea where to look, we were able to get a feel for it when we partially reamed a few holes and then carefully measured. Looking at the position of where the reamer started told the story in every hole. Once again, counting failures hides the story. Characterizing **System Behavior** might be as simple as a cartoon as long as the proper question is asked!

This was not a difficult project, but flawed models hid the truth. The truth was not in the data, but in the observations of the **System Behavior**. All we needed was a chair and a drawing to ask a simple question: "What is happening?"

Years later, there I was, once again crawling around a factory that made batteries – drawing a sketch – this time with a new heart and my Chinese team member who became my good friend.

"What are you looking for?" he asked, thinking I was taking too long after 15 minutes of looking and drawing. We had much of what we needed so we went to a room with a whiteboard.

"Your boss handed me 18 months of data that jammed my computer, which is my fault. I should have known better than to load it. The entire 18 months of data has no physical relationship whatsoever to machine function and **System Behavior**. Worse, I can't see the original values since they took averages of seven readings across the web. The first thing we need is to define a cycle, the starting point for decomposing **System Behavior**."

"There is no cycle. It is a continuous operation. One cycle," he said, "is thousands of meters of foil."

"That is never true and let me show you why."

There is a positive displacement screw pump that draws the slurry from a holding tank, then pushes it through a filter and to a slot die, which lays down the slurry onto the web as the web is pulled through the die. I was also interested in the pump performance curve because I could see that the filters were changed frequently, but that is for another chapter. The operator was making pump speed adjustments based on averages of a measurement system I did not yet trust. The speed adjustments were necessary because as the filter got clogged, flow was impeded. The 18 months of data was worthless to me because none of it could be related to function based on a proper cycle. It also provided no indication at all as to when and why adjustments were made and the effect of making them.

I checked the angular velocity of the screw pump in revolutions per minute, then calculated that 0.6 meters of web are coated in one revolution. That defines one cycle. The problem had been defined as *Process Capability*, which is not a question. A superior and more effective approach would be:

1. How much of the tolerance is used to create one machine cycle?
2. If the system cycles once more, does the second cycle look like the first?

You don't need 18 months of data over thousands of meters! In less than two meters you can get plenty of insight into what is happening. Then do it again in a logical interval if called for, such as the beginning and end of the slurry reservoir. Intervals must be based on machine cycles, not time.

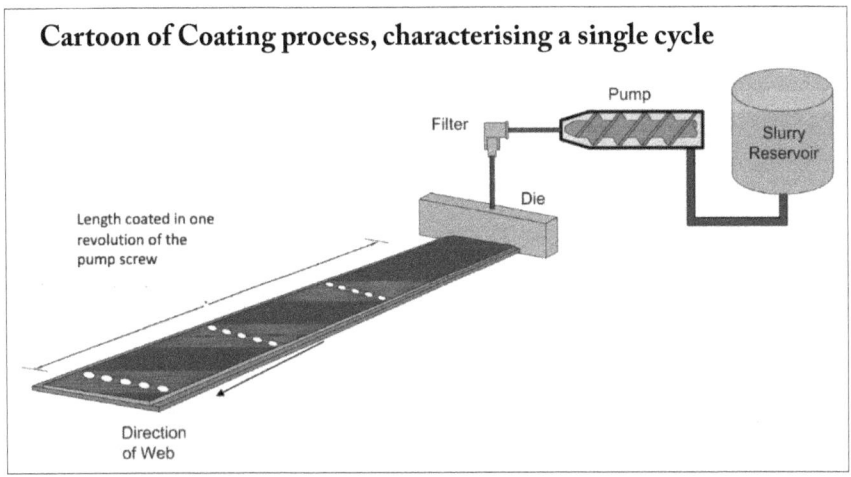

Figure 3-2

Typically, each cycle would have three measurements across the web at three intervals for three cycles. I was curious as to the slot die performance, thus I took five measurements across the web. The client was taking seven, which I knew was too many, and averaging away the differences, which was precisely the insight we needed. The thinking was that to get a better average, get more values. That makes no sense if what we need is lost once you average away the truth.

Instead of falling into the flawed model of common cause-special cause, start with the fact that the model for **Small Multiples** for characterizing **System Behavior**, if properly done, readily reveals:

- Information about machine performance, which drives process characteristics, is always carried on the outputs of a process cycle.
- Start by defining a cycle. The cycle contains the datum reference frame and is directly a function of machine periodicity.
- Decompose into sub-cycles.
- Do not sample to see super cycles until you have observed serial cycles. Most often, you will have already seen everything you need.

- Plot the results as you get it. Don't collect a bunch of data and then plot it. Start on a whiteboard so you and your team can learn as you plot.

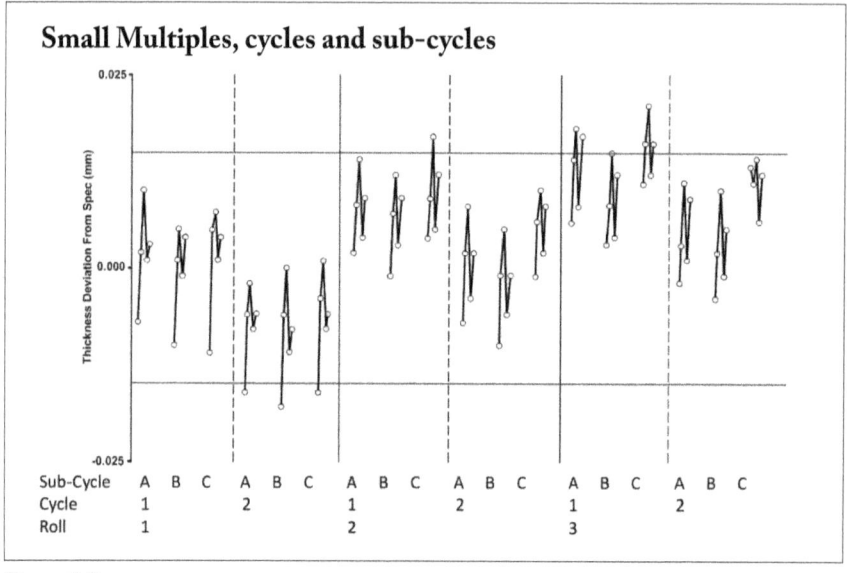

Figure 3-3

- Most of the tolerance is used up in a single cycle.
- Half the tolerance was used up across the web in a single sub-cycle. The company was blind to the most important part of the story because of averages.
- If you are using more than half the tolerance for sub-cycles and cycles, there is nothing left for super-cycles. The good news is that the Causal Explanation is usually quite simple.
- The principle adjustment for the operator controlling coating weight was slurry pump speed, which, as mentioned, decreased once the filter became blocked and impeded flow. Adjusting pump speed did increase the coating weight somewhat uniformly, but cross-web variation was such that it was easy to go out of spec, but we were blinded by averages.

The lack of uniformity across the web, which we captured as a sub-cycle, was principally a function of the slot die. The procedure for setting the slot die was so complicated that it was set and then ignored. Once we knew what was really needed it was not difficult to fix it.

We started with a cartoon to begin to understand the dynamics of **System Behavior**. Small observations taken multiple times, called **Small Multiples,** provided insight into the machine action that created the feature we care about (coating weight), allowing us to answer the question "What is happening?" If you are beginning to think, "This is just common sense," then you are right where you should be!

The starting point for this project was the quality control model for *Process Capability*. A far more insightful way is to start with a cartoon, figure out what a cycle is, then see how much of the allotted variation is used up in a single cycle. This view assigns observed variation to how the process actually works, as opposed to short-term and long-term variation based on time and a flawed probabilistic sampling plan. Observations must be directly associated with *what is happening* based on the physics of a cycle – simple and powerful.

Calendaring

The results of our work were shown to the quality manager with hardly more than a day or two into the project.

"The calendering machine is supposed to smooth out the coating. Your results don't show the true performance."

"Maybe," I thought to myself.

The calendering machine is two large, highly polished steel rolls between which the web is passed under high pressure, creating a concentrated force. The idea is to compress the coating to increase the density. The measurement system is different from the coating weight. The value reported is the thickness, not a weight converted to a value per square meter. This measurement system really does measure thickness, using a non-contact electronic system that is quite repeatable. Checking it was a bit tricky because the variation in a small area can easily be confounded with measurement error if you are not careful.

Once again, every project starts with a question that helps gain insight and progresses to the next question. The coating project required decomposing variation by cycles, sub-cycles, and then, if necessary, super-cycles. The same thing is true at calendaring.

One calendaring role is a bit larger than the other so as they rotate, the line of contact, or mating location, changes each time around. We defined a cycle as a single rotation of the larger of the two rolls – the circumference: 1.8 meters.

Proper characterization of **System Behavior** requires that we measure a section of web that was measured after coating, measure it again with the non-contact device, then once again after calendaring, then compared.

How much should we run? Well, the guidelines indicate 1.8 meters × 3 cycles, or just under 6 meters.

The specific question was "Does the calendering machine even out the surface thickness differences that are created in each sub-cycle of the coating process?"

The general model of isolation asks, "Is the output a result of the function of the machine, or the input to the machine?

In this case, we needed to know if the web retained the fundamental shape characteristics after calendaring, or does the calendering machine impose its own pattern? Another way to say it is: Is the output dependent on the input or the function?

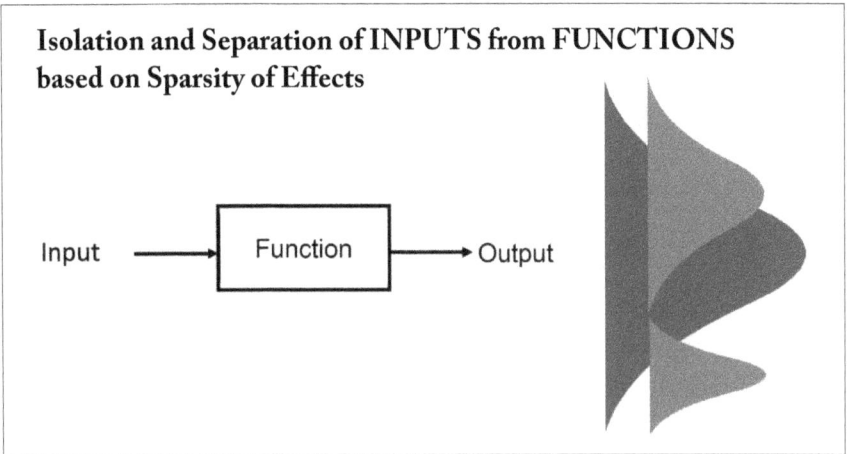

Figure 3-4

We chose to run about two meters through the calendering machine to keep things simple and not gum up production. This merits a word: Once you can effectively characterize **System Behavior** and learn to ask serial questions, sample sizes will become small once you gain confidence. Once you ask for access to a machine for a test, and tell those with the power to grant access that you are going to run a few meters instead of a several kilometers, the answer will be, "Sure, go ahead," instead of "We can slot you in next month."

In this case, six meters was all we needed to get quite interesting results. The calendering machine does just as intended: compressing the coating to increase the density. However, the pattern imposed by the coating machine was still clearly there! The calendering machine compresses the coating, but cannot smear it around to reduce thickness variation. The pattern of thickness measurements are nearly identical before and after calendaring. The values are reduced as it is compressed. Therefore, the observed variation measured after calendaring is because of the input to calendaring, not the function of calendaring.

If we want better thickness control we have to do it on the coating line, and the **Small Multiples** tells us right where to do it: the slot die.

Matryoshka, The Story Within the Story

Matryoshka-Small Multiples is simple and eye-opening. The key learning point is that we want to look at what happens within a cycle. When you change the question to "What is happening," it means *right now*!

When you think of variation as random, and a function of chance across time, you are setting yourself up to get confused because the model is not helpful for characterizing **System Behavior**. The beauty of **Small Multiples** based on cycles, sub-cycles, and super-cycles in a manufacturing process is that the variation you carefully capture with only a few samples can be attributed to a specific machine function. Patterns associated with that function are easy to see and associate with that function, and simple to fix.

We have a thumb rule for **Small Multiples**. You should be able to produce five serial cycles without using more than half the tolerance, and keep it centered. That leaves the necessary margin for super-cycle variation and will pass any capability study you are asked to perform. Once again, start with one cycle! And do not average away the differences that often live in the story of the smallest doll.

This model for characterizing **System Behavior** is far more meaningful than *Process Capability* because it calls for a datum framework based on the dynamics of machine function and measurements taken in such a way as to reveal the nature of the process. It starts with the assumption that manufacturing is not a random number generator, although it might look like one with a sampling plan that thinks of it as a Black Box.

The critical nature of manufacturing today and the demands on precision and repeatability require you to look inside the Black Box and force it to reveal its nature.

Battery performance today, demonstrated in the previous example, is such that the consequences of manufacturing mistakes are severe. The old ways of looking at performance and reliability are not good enough. Look closely at your models. Question them. We do! Improve them where you can, and change them when necessary. It really is simple. The only thing that might be standing in the way are your models.

Face Up to Measurements

Observe Data Collection at the Moment of Measurement

See, observe, learn how data are collected at the moment and place of measurement. "You never learn more about a process than when you directly observe how data are measured," said Cuthbert Daniel, a superb applied statistician. See with fresh eyes. Wall around what you want to learn about. Talk to those who do the measurements. See how numbers came to be.

—Edward Tufte

Chapter 4

Seeing with Fresh Eyes

Edward Tufte's[1] books are among the most important and influential not only in our creation and application of Matryoshka Small Multiples, but also in everything we do. His most recent book, *Seeing with Fresh Eyes*, makes me think that we have merely scratched the surface of what is possible. It also reminds us how easy it is to be blinded by massive data, collected based on flawed or misapplied models.

One of the first projects I worked on as a consultant was at a steel mill in California. I took the assignment when a friend asked me to help. I agreed, thinking I would do it for a while, then get a real job. That was half a lifetime ago. The mill imported bands of steel from an Asian supplier that were processed through a 5-stand mill to reduce the thickness from about 8-10 millimeters down to sizes as thin as soup cans. It was a fascinating process, as the steel was pulled like taffy in several serial steps. The high-speed process was such that a break or tear in the steel resulted in a mess that could take a day or more to sort out, with the precision steel rolls severely damaged as well.

---

1 Seeing with Fresh Eyes: Meaning, Space, Data, Truth, Edward Tufte, 2020
Visual Explanations: Images, Quantities, Evidence and Narrative, Edward R. Tufte, 1997

Processed steel was used to make tinned cans for food as well as zinc-coated pipes for drainage ditches. The zinc was melted in a large vat. The steel came off a large roll then into a series of loops to manage the slack, called a festoon, then into an acid bath to pickle and clean, then into the zinc, or galvanizing bath, in another large loop. As it came out, there was an air knife to blow excess zinc back down into the bath and provide a uniform coating… sort of. From there, the steel went into a furnace to bond the zinc to the steel. The furnace was another large series of loops that went from below the ground to above the roof.

The seasonal demand for the product was such that the line ran 24 hours a day, seven days a week. The zinc specification called for a minimum spec, with no upper limit. The company was giving away zinc, because the risk of going below the specification, they thought, was substantial. There were two separate measurement systems. The one that was trusted was similar to the anode coating. Disks were punched and weighed, the zinc was stripped off with acid and then weighed again, and the amount of zinc was calculated. The process is called weigh-strip-weigh (WSW.) The calculation provided the combined zinc weight on both sides of the steel. WSW was a standard and had to be followed. Because of the way it was used, a fortune in zinc was given away.

The zigzag pattern above represents the second measurement, an online system. It was a clever device with a source of radiation on top of the strip and a receiver on the opposite side. The scanner was mounted on a ball screw that constantly went back and forth. The speed at which the scanner went back and forth was independent of the speed of the steel. Consequently, the zigzag pattern was hard to use to diagnose much of anything.

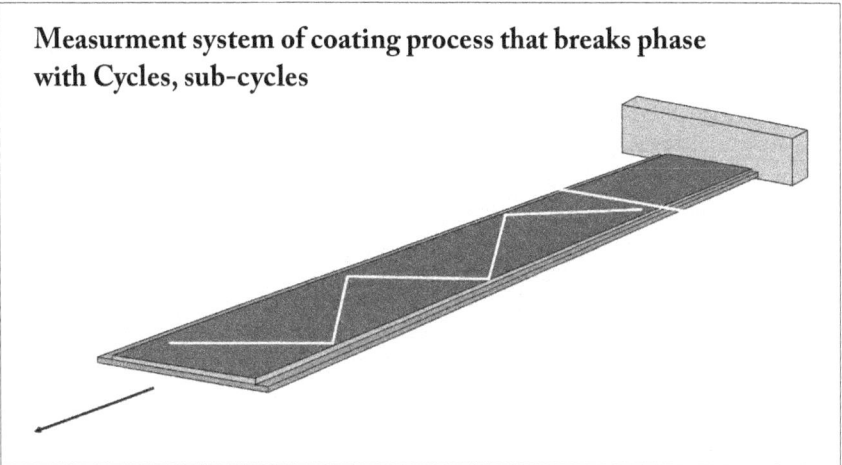

Figure 4-1

This was where things got interesting. The air knives were supposed to control the thickness of the zinc coating from edge to edge and from side to side on the opposite sides. The WSW at the end of the line was fine for inspection; but, as we said, it was giving away zinc. The scanner was a clever device, but missed the mark as it logged data that was observed but not used.

At that point in life, I had never heard of **Small Multiples**, sub-cycles, or smallest effective difference. I did know how important it was to take good notes and make sketches. Then again, maybe I was lucky and learned to sketch and take notes because PowerPoint and digital cameras had not been invented!

I did know that the scanner had potential that was not being used, which could mean huge savings. Instead of running the scanner constantly back and forth, it was programmed to move to a position near one edge of the steel and stop for a few seconds. Now we could see the difference from top to bottom, as well as the variation within a line along the steel a meter or so long. The principle of **Small Multiples** was being applied. The scanner then moved to the center, stopped, logged meaningful values that provided the ability to see the smallest effective differences, then moved to the far side and did it again. After a bit of practice we were able to adjust the air knives to manage the coating economically, and use the WSW to make sure we met the specification. This was my first consulting project where simplicity saved a fortune.

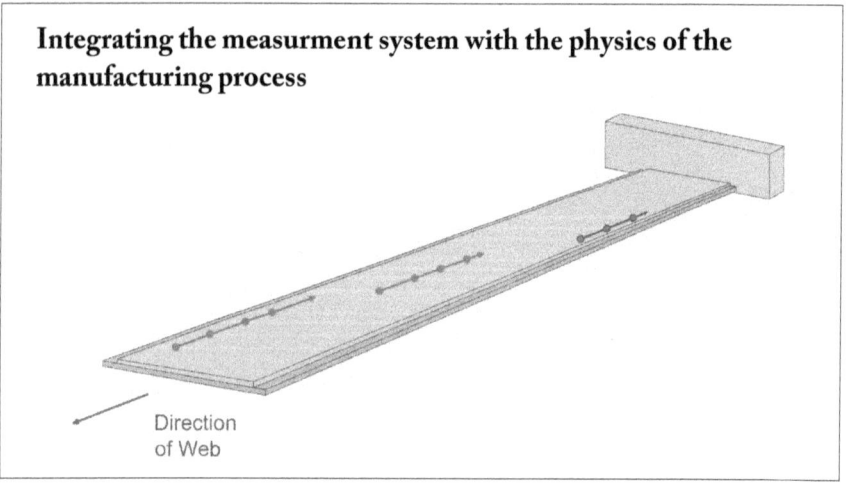

FIGURE 4-2

The technical sophistication of such scanners has improved since this project was in place. However, some are too sophisticated by half. Sheets of light are used in extruding tire treads that log terabytes of data when a dial indicator might be a good start to see what is happening in a single cycle. The dial indicator makes us think through what we need and how to get it, as opposed to logging expensive data and then figuring out how to analyze it from your home office. Remember, data has to be turned into information, then knowledge – that is your job!

Wind Turbines

I worked on several projects at a wind turbine gearbox manufacturer in China.

One was for an inspection cover for the gearbox that leaked oil and ran down the housing. I asked a young technician to measure the shape, which was visibly distorted by welding on the handles. You could actually put it on the floor and step on one side and see it wobble. Once the cover warped, the bolts to hold it down did not just compress the gasket, but instead wasted effort in straining the cover, thus resulting in leaks. The torque spec was met but the effort was wasted on straining the cover, not compressing the gasket. You now know they measure only one of the conjugate variables! Torque alone only tells half the story.

I asked the technician to set the cover on three cones and use a dial indicator to check it in 12 positions, which I marked. Then I asked him to provide me with the numbers so I could make a simple sketch on a whiteboard.

There was no dial indicator. There were no cones. There was no surface plate in inspection. He mounted the cover in a holding fixture, wrote a program to scan it, and proudly handed me a thumb drive with a long list of numbers and a single calculation for flatness. I could have taken the numbers and put them into Excel, but why? What we needed was a whiteboard and a few numbers with no calculations! We were blind to the simple truth by data! A dial indicator could tell the story where the Coordinate Measuring Machine (CMM) failed because it collected a mountain of data not turned into information.

To think your way through such problems, you always need to figure out what you want to see, how a product or process will reveal it, and the most simple way to get the observations. The things we can do with machines these days are amazing. However, the smarter the machines we invent, the more clever we have to think to use them properly to characterize

System Behavior. Brilliant machines allow us to do so much more – they also provide every chance to be foolish. That is the challenge! We all need to see with fresh eyes to meet the demands of today.

Leaf Springs

A leaf spring in a popular vehicle was cracking, with plenty of blame to go around; but no one had figured out what was happening. The rare failure mode, cracks (the outermost Matryoshka doll), was where the story was thought to unfold. You now know the failure mode is merely evidence of physics that is ubiquitous.

A list was made of everything that could possibly go wrong, many of the things on the list coming from people behind desks thousands of miles and time zones away who had never seen the process. The team never asked, "What is wrong?" The time for that had passed. That is a question for the experts, but they could not find the answer. We needed a system for discovery and **Dynamic Learning** that was fast and innovative. We characterized the **System Behavior** of the manufacturing process and the failures. It took two weeks in India. This project was especially interesting. The first time I saw the springs was in Houston, Texas, after the container was offloaded. The supplier claimed they were all *good* when they were shipped. Such a flawed conclusion can generate actions that lead nowhere. There were only a few broken in Houston, but by then we knew that every single one was at risk!

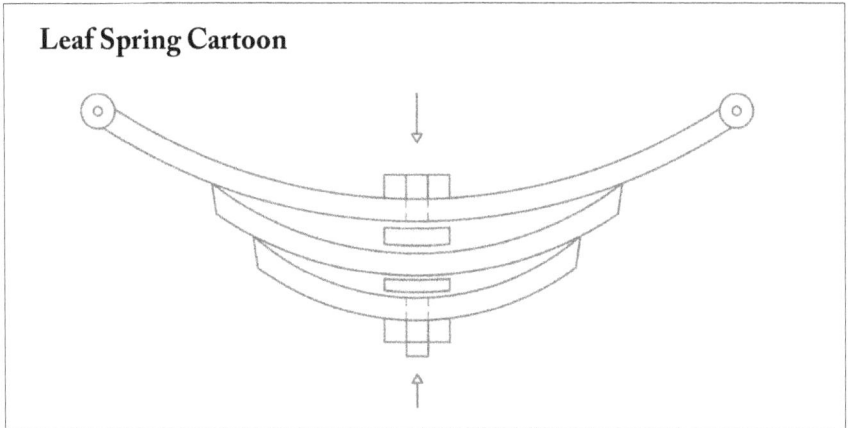

Figure 4-3

An early observation was that only the top spring in the stack was broken and that the break always started at the bottom of the pierced through-hole where a bolt held it all together. The offending leaf, like all the others, was pierced in a press, tearing the steel on the strained side. Every leaf was exposed to the same treatment in the factory from piercing to heat-treat and forming. Any and all of the proposed *root causes* from afar did not fit the evidence. One theory was quench cracks. How could that be if every leaf went through the quench tank but only the top leaf cracked and never until arrival in Houston? Why did only the top leaf fail when there was no difference in the manufacturing process? We had to explain the difference.

There was a zinc-plated spacer between the leaves to keep them separated so they didn't rub and make noise. The cartoon helps us think and see, forcing us to pay attention to details that are easy to miss. The zinc spacer was interesting. Zinc is often used as a sacrificial anode and yields hydrogen in an electrolytic reaction if you add a bit of seawater. My cartoon showed corrosion on the cracked parts in Houston. (Everyone who owns a boat knows this.) The clues were documented carefully in my notebook, and I was off to India. If hydrogen can find a way into steel through a fracture or a tear, the forces are tremendous. Tears could possibly provide access for hydrogen, especially if strained on the side with tears.[2]

The spring manufacturer was on the southeast coast on the Bay of Bengal. It was hot and humid outside and worse in the plant. I had a look-around, but had a feel for what I wanted to see.

I had a hard time watching the pressing operation. The press operator wore flip-flops and had to use makeshift tools to clear stuck parts after each cycle. Because every part stuck in the piercing operation, the safety mechanisms had been defeated. It made the hair stand up on the back of my neck.

> I have been fortunate to have worked in many cultures around the world. The contributions I have made are no match for the lessons generously shared with me by so many. It was well after noon one day in India when I said to my team member, "I am starving. Let's go eat." It seemed well out of character for one of the kindest men I ever met to point his finger at me and abruptly say, "You have no idea what starving is. Look around you. You are just hungry." I think of his lesson every time I am merely hungry and think I am starving.

As previously mentioned tears could possibly provide access for hydrogen. Figure 4-4 shows the load-pattern for the top-leaf versus the two bottom leaves; but this load-pattern was while the spring was in the unloaded state. Once it was installed into a vehicle, the top-spring load-pattern reversed, and theoretically removed the risk. On the top-leaf, the exit of the pierced hole is in tension while the top is in compression – while in the two bottom leaves, the pattern is reversed, so the exit hole is in compression.

---

[2] This was not the first project we had worked on where hydrogen caused such damage. My notes, piled in my office, are an excellent reference, although not as good as David's notes. He never throws anything away. David wrote an excellent chemical summary of this project in Diagnosing Performance and Reliability after the project was finished.

You can see this in Figure 4-3. This fit the clues that we needed in order to prove we knew what we were talking about.

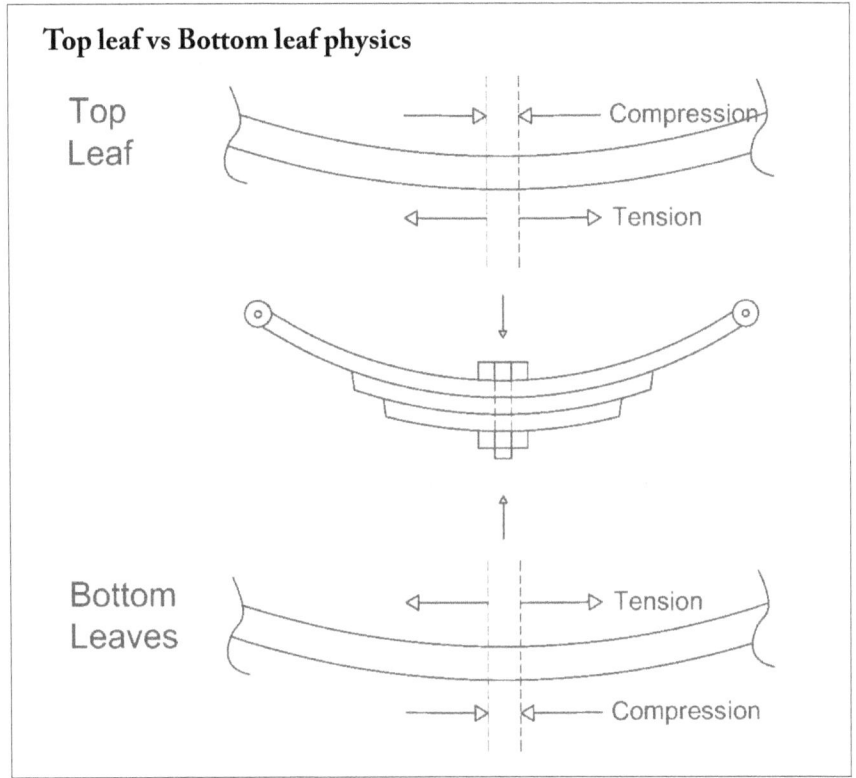

Figure 4-4

Our small team managed to find a *plater* a short distance away who was willing to allow us to dip a few leaves into an acid bath with a bag of zinc to generate hydrogen. The hydrogen made the bath bubble up like a witches' brew. I kept an eye out for smokers. As I looked about, I noticed a few cows eating the weeds around the fence not far from the acid bath.

Once we got the test parts back to the factory, we built a fixture to strain the offending top-leaf at the through-hole, hooked up two 12 volt batteries in series across the system with a grounded zinc spacer between them, and had a worker pour saltwater over it every hour or so. By morning, eight of the 12 parts had cracked just as they had in Houston. Once again, every part was at risk. Finding cracks might have been a rare event, but once the physics were understood, the story unfolded. To really see what was happening, we just had to turn up the volume, which you can only do once you understand it. Not a single cracked part had been found at the manufacturer; but once loaded into a container and then onto a ship, everything needed to set off the reaction was present: a tear in the metal, one strained side, a salty, moist, and humid atmosphere, and a zinc spacer!

One engineer argued that my test was flawed because the source of hydrogen was exaggerated. He had a hard time believing the corrosion would happen so fast, and that every single one was at risk. It took a bit of time, and he got it. The fix was simple. Stop piercing the holes for all the leaves, and ripping the steel as the tool exited the part, providing a home for the hydrogen. Controlling variation would not have worked. The operation had to be changed to a new way; but I didn't want to watch. Once again, only a few were reported as failures, while every single one was at risk. These are not statistics problems, but physics problems! Your customers deserve performance, and you deserve to know how to ask effective questions and get answers... quickly.

Upon completion of this project the plant manager asked me if I would teach his engineers. I told him that I would be happy to do so, once he made changes so that every person could work in safety and dignity.

> *The people who are crazy enough to think they can change the world are the ones who do.*
>
> **—Steve Jobs**

Chapter 5

Source Load, Effort, and Flow

Several years ago, before we had really documented the principles of characterizing **System Behavior**, we were called to a company because, they said, the brakes on a car were failing at the assembly plant in the hold-yard, which just means they were outside in the weather just before shipping.

"We have 100 percent pass at the end of the assembly line. After a few days in the hold-lot, we have a small number of vehicles where the brakes fail. The pedal goes to the floor, but only once. There are no subsequent failures. We think it has something to do with the cold weather."

This is a perfect example of well-meaning people getting confused because of the way they defined the problem. Once again, they thought this was a rare event where some complex combination of variables all lined up to interact, making it difficult to find the cause. It is not uncommon for people to get confused when thinking in terms of probabilistic interactions and flawed problem definitions. The deterministic model of **Source-Load** and **First Principles** is simpler and more revealing.

Although we did not have a documented learning map then, we knew:

- Characterize System Behavior by changing the question.

- If one single system fails, assume that all are at risk until you can prove otherwise.
- Assume physics is present in all of them! Looking for the difference between good and bad will not lead to the Causal Explanation your company needs.
- Just because they all pass, your knowledge is still meager and unsatisfactory and will be until you characterize System Behavior.

A simple whiteboard cartoon revealed that a manifold with valves and solenoids triggered by sensors and powered by 12 volts comprised the heart of the system. Once again, we wanted to know how well the system worked – not just if it worked. In order to do so, we needed a power supply to manipulate the effort to shuttle the solenoids. The battery in the vehicle only provided a constant 12 volts. How much effort does it take to shuttle the solenoids? As we manipulated the effort, we needed to know the flow, which is when the solenoid shuttles. You couldn't see the shuttle, so we decided to get a stethoscope from a medical supply company. I wasn't so much interested in if the brakes failed, but rather characterizing and understanding the **System Behavior** and functions required for the brakes to work by finding the Effort (voltage) when the solenoid shuttled the valve.

At this point, the power supply was hooked up to the manifold, and the battery was disconnected using vehicles from the end of the line. Every single solenoid shuttled when just 3-4 volts were applied. Since the battery supplied 12 volts, there was certainly plenty of margin.

The test rig was moved outside, where it was cold and windy and I had only a light jacket – so I wanted to move quickly. Every vehicle we tested in the yard needed at least 6 volts to shuttle. A few would not shuttle even with 20 volts, which was the limit of the power supply. The majority, which did shuttle at a higher voltage, shuttled each subsequent test at a much lower voltage.

Our new knowledge and insight was documented on the whiteboard. A whiteboard for me, as well as for David and Tobias, has become not only a place to write but a place to collectively organize our thoughts and test our ability to explain them. If the voltage to make the solenoid shuttle was between 6 and 12 volts, the vehicle would have been declared good. All we would know is that the brakes worked, not how well. But we knew something was amiss, because the same vehicles at the end of the assembly line shuttled at 3-4 volts. Every vehicle that needed more than 12 volts would have been declared a failure. In vehicles brought back into the building and left for 24 hours, the effort to shuttle went back to 3-4 volts. The difficulty was that subsequent tries masked the problem. We needed to see it on the first try, and we had to do it outside in the cold.

We now knew that every single vehicle was at risk, and the flawed thinking of just good versus bad impedes effective problem solving, presenting a *Hobson's choice*[1].

We found a couple of vehicles that needed more than 20 volts, and carefully took them apart. There was evidence of crystals on the solenoid valve that looked like salt.

With a bit of research we discovered that a certain kind of brake fluid reacts with rust inhibitors to form what looks like salt crystals. The company that made the solenoid valves and manifolds on another continent suddenly decided it was a good idea to be extra careful and use the rust inhibitor prior to shipping. It was easily cleaned off the manifold, but the solenoids were powdered metal so the rust inhibitor could not be fully removed. With such an understanding, we could either find an alternative to the rust inhibitor or change the type of brake fluid. A **Causal Explanation** provided the ability to take proper and responsible action and to completely eliminate the problem.

The story became clear once we had an effective way to see!

---

[1] Hobson's choice is the illusion that multiple choices are available, when it is really "take it or leave it."

Now you know how important it is to think in terms of **System Behavior** as a starting point. The **Source-Load** model provides insight into behavior, providing an effective way to see what is happening with the flow of energy and power, avoiding the probabilistic pitfalls of good vs. bad.

What do you think the potential for real improvement would be if we characterized **System Behavior** before we sold a single one? Do you think you would gain real insight into performance and reliability? What problems have you worked on where such an approach might have helped you, as well as your company?

You also know the importance we place on effective models. The **Universal Source-Load** model is where we would begin. It is worth noting that this was a mental model before we wrote it down. We learned how it was important to expand the model into serial and parallel functions as needed. We also learned to label conjugate variables, and the importance of conversions from domain to domain, and transmissions where we account for losses within a domain to see the full story.

We learned how to plot on the effort-flow workspace providing a graphical representation of what is really happening. We learned to manipulate the load lines to sweep, as much as we can, from axis to axis, revealing hidden performance truths.

We cannot overemphasize what you are missing when selecting some tool that only works with a single Y response variable instead of the effort-flow conjugate pair.

Split Brake Lines

A midwestern US company called because of the performance of a tube-bending machine. Straight tubes were supplied to the machine then formed to shape for brake tubing for trucks. The machine had been purchased and tested to run-at-rate at the machine builder, then shipped and was paid. It passed with flying colors. It wasn't a fair test. The buyer should have known, or at least been advised as to the risks of such a machine.

There were several bends in each tube so it would fit in the truck. Each was performed by extending a separate air cylinder. The bends were all performed in series. The first bend was initiated by a start button. Each serial bend was based on a timer timing out, which was assumed to be enough time for the piston that was performing a bend to complete its task. As the timer timed out, the next bend was initiated. If the next bend was initiated before the tubing was in its proper position on the mandrel, the bend could create a kink or a fracture, which is the reason we were called. Brake lines were leaking. This caused the truck manufacturer to get a bit excited.

The supplier run-at-rate test was with an air supply adjacent to the machine and clean new cylinders. At the plant, the air supply was remote. The air pressure at the bending machine would be a function of other factory loads. It is if you are taking a hot shower on the second floor of your house and someone decides to water the flowers outside, starving the cold water and scalding you.

There was one single air manifold. The logic opened and shut the valves to the air cylinders based on the sequence and timers. From the single manifold were rubber hoses, some quite long, some with splices and hose clamps, a poor substitute for rigid pipes. Now we know the air supply was at risk, and that the displacement was a function of the effort or pressure. That's not all!

What happens when the piston rods are not lubricated? It gets worse.

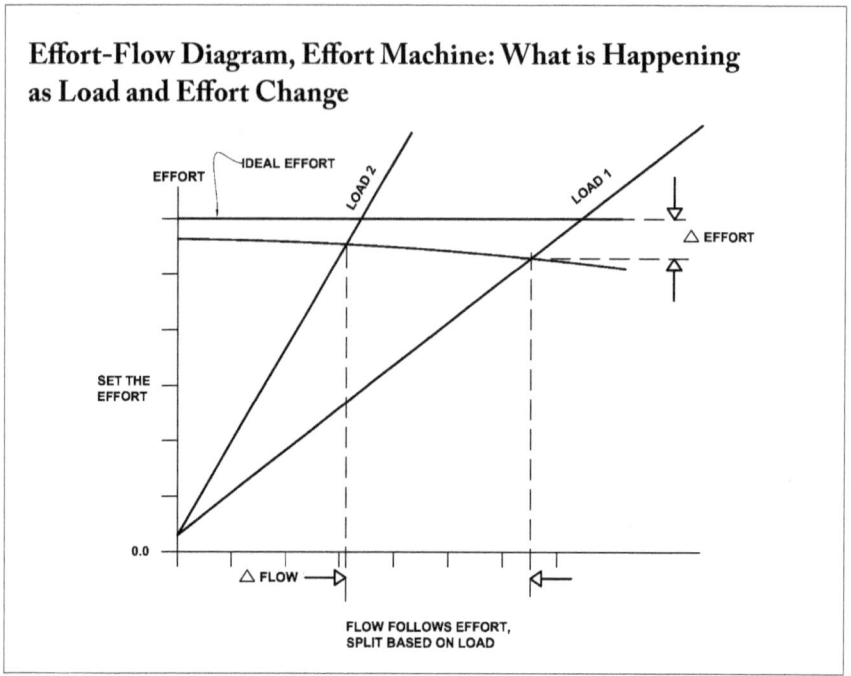

Figure 5-1

On the whiteboard, I drew Figure 5-1. If we hope to operate at the intersection of the Load 1 line and the Effort 1, which is just below the Ideal Effort line, the tube bender would operate at the high end of the horizontal flow axis. If, for example, the pistons lacked lubricant then the system load would shift to Load 2 but still on Effort Line 1. The pressure change is minimal, and the tube bender would slow down and operate at the lower end of the horizontal flow axis, and at risk of damaging tubes.

The broken line that is labeled Effort 2 is what would happen if the air pressure dropped. The intersection of Load 1 and Effort 2 is still at risk. If the pistons were fouled, for example, and the air pressure were at Effort 2, the velocity would drop even lower on the horizontal axis. Given that we know the rubber hoses are a poor substitute for copper or steel pipes, and that the air compressor was too far away, the system effort would move up and down the vertical axis, creating havoc.

Flow Based

If we replace the air cylinders by electrically operated actuators we would create a flow-based machine. Why? The actuators would be supplied by volts and amps. The effort would still be torque and the flow, displacement or velocity. This is represented on Figure 5-2. The actuators, by their nature, respond to changes in the load. If the load increases, then the actuator draws more current thus increasing the torque. It simply pushes harder, essentially at the same velocity. Effort-based air cylinders do not respond to the load. They just push until equilibrium is reached, slowing down and ultimately stopping.

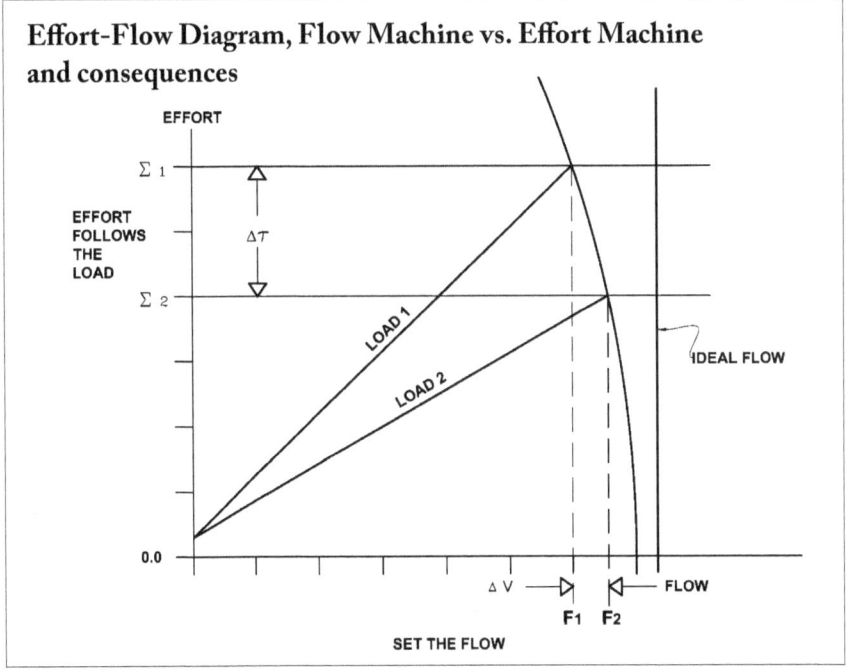

Figure 5-2

We would likely set up the machine in 5-2 to operate the intersection of the Load 2 line and the real flow line. If the load increases to Line 1, the operating point would shift along the real flow line and the torque would increase up the vertical axis in response. As the effort increases, there is only a small change in flow. Such a machine provides consistent results.

The plant manager at the brake tube plant said they had considered such a machine (flow-based) but it was more expensive. I said nothing. But I wanted to make a list.

- Air is more expensive than electricity.
- The cost of detecting leaks while selling at-risk tubes adds up fast. The cost of finding and removing them once in the field could be backbreaking.
- It is easy and inexpensive to monitor volts and amps, but not pressure and volumetric flow
- Customer visits, airline tickets, travel, and subsequent help from consultants is expensive.
- Frustration, stress and anxiety adds up because of a marginal decision, mostly for the people in the factory who get more than their fair share of the blame.
- If a single leaking tube was sold, there are a lot more at risk.
- Selling at-risk products is likely the single most costly quality event from an economic standpoint as well as the damage it causes to brand value. You just cannot recover the losses.

Rubber hoses were replaced with rigid pipe. An air tank was installed close to the load, and the cylinders cleaned and lubricated according to a schedule. The timers were set slightly slower. It worked; but the machine had to be run a bit slower, but not so much that production needs could not be met.

Performance at t_0 and t_n

A brand new extruder just arrived at the factory, was bolted to the floor, plumbed and wired. Production demands are such that your team has been working around the clock to get it running. The team got it running with a bit of pressure from senior management, and it seems to be meeting the demand. Arriving at work at 7AM the day after startup, you are pleased to see it running and producing well. You get a coffee and go to your office with one other person from the team.

"How do we know this new machine is performing well?" you ask.

"Because it is producing material," he replies.

You know that is not good enough, so you step to the whiteboard and begin to reproduce Figure 5-2 based on what you learned from a workshop John, David and Tobias from Crossover Solutions helped with a few months ago.

You want to draw the generalized effort-flow representation for the extruder. You draw and label the vertical axis torque, and the horizontal axis angular velocity of the screw. You draw the vertical ideal flow line and a characteristic curve for the extruder. You draw two load lines and are pleased. What you drew looks just like Figure 5-2

The effort-flow performance is a powerful means to monitor **System Behavior** starting when a machine is new. The characteristic curve should be close to the ideal flow line at the point of sale, meaning the losses are minimal. As the system ages, you explain to your team member, the characteristic curve will lean more to the left and the area between the curve and the ideal line will increase. The area represents the total system losses. You want to know where the curve is for the brand new machine and want a plan to monitor performance as it decays, which you know it will because of system entropy[2]. You have been around for a while and know

---

[2] Entropy – a thermodynamic quantity representing the unavailability or losses of a systems energy for conversion to useful work due to a gradual decline into disorder.

the clearance between the screw and barrel will increase. The velocity of the machine might be increased to compensate but you know it will cost more to power the huge motor. In the past you just took out the screw and measured it. This time, you want to plot the performance on the effort-flow workspace. All you need to get started is a current probe to measure and data log the motor current and the angular velocity of the screw and a calculator to multiply them together to get the kW.

You do not quite know what to expect, but you get some values. You leave your team member at the machine and go back to the whiteboard, but only plot a single point, which isn't really very interesting. A few moments later, your team member comes in with a few more paired values. You plot them and notice there are enough to connect them and draw a characteristic curve, dropping it to the axis. What happened? A decrease in the compliance of the extruded material. The batches of raw material to the extruder were from a different lot, changing the load, so you draw load lines from each point to the origin. After lunch, the die is changed for a new extrusion. The angular velocity for the new part is decreased so you draw a vertical line from the horizontal axis. You plot a few more points and are pleased with how much you learned with so little effort. You step back and have drawn Figure 5-3.

You add the broken line, T_n, with the intent to have a look again after a month or so to see if the system performance has decayed since the installation.

This is simple so you decide to do one more plot of pressure versus volumetric flow, which, you realize, should yield the ability to calculate power in kW per kg of processed material. This gives you the idea to look at another extruder, which you discover takes 25 percent more power per kg.

These simple plots provide real and valuable insight into **System Behavior**. With just a few points you have the answer to the most fundamental question in performance and reliability engineering:

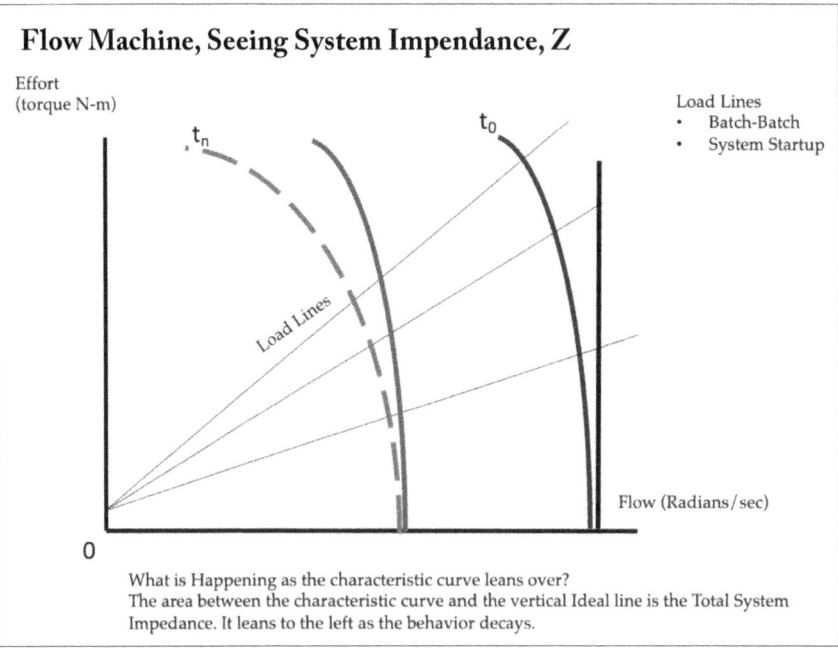

FIGURE 5-3

How Well Does it Work?

Characterizing **System Behavior** answers that question. Run-at-rate is a test that suffers the flaw of pass-fail, and is how the tube bender company got into trouble.

Effort-Based Machines and the Consequences

Effort-based machines have their place and are perfect for many applications. We have been examining the consequences of using air-operated, effort-based machines when perhaps flow-based machines should have been considered. Centrifugal pumps are effort-based and used for everything from massive coolant pumps to heart pumps. You certainly would not want a flow-based pump to provide water to your house! Where the effort-based centrifugal pump maintains pressure and stops the flow, a flow-based positive displacement pump would maintain the flow once you shut the water off, blowing the pipes apart.

There is a new effort-based mechanical heart pump I read about in August 2024. The pump uses magnetic levitation principles instead of bearings. That's interesting on two levels. The characteristic curve would be nearly vertical. Since the system losses are so low, the power requirements are low as well. The present pumps are larger with journal bearings, and have larger external batteries that need to be recharged daily. The battery for this new smaller pump will still need to be charged daily but the external battery pack will be small. Also interesting, a centrifugal heart pump provides no pulse since the flow is constant. The new pump will save lives for those waiting for heart transplants.

The Broken Coil Wire

A company that made all kinds of electronic devices and components called us with an interesting problem. They knew precisely what was wrong with the coil they were making for an anti-lock braking system! I don't recall another example in over 40 years of being told what was wrong, knowing where the problem occurred, but not knowing how to make it stop. Figure 10 in the Appendix shows a sketch. There is a terminal inserted by a high-speed machine. The terminal periodically cuts the wire during the insertion process. The fault is not detectable by simple and fast circuit tests; however, once the parts are installed into the ABS system, there are reported failures in the field. The brakes work, but the ABS system fails, and it can be thousands of miles or kilometers before the connection fails even though it is cut. In an effort to find cut wires, the company bought an expensive x-ray machine for 100 percent inspection. Of course, it was expensive. And, of course, it wasn't close to 100 percent effective.

The problem is detection at the source. The cycle time for the machine building the coils was about one second, and there were several parallel machines. For as many years and as many factories I have visited, it still amazes me that so many things can be produced so fast and customers often cannot get enough of them. As soon as I saw the insertion machine, I knew this project would not take long. The terminal was inserted by a linear actuator. This is a flow-based machine, and it was easy to hook up a current probe and data logger.

Mounted, Polished picture, wire severed by bobbin during insertion

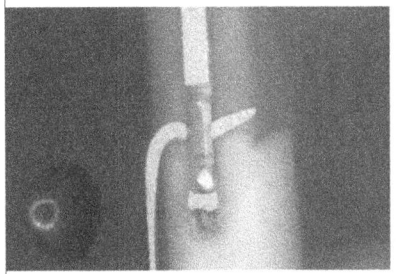

The picture in 5-4 is a mounted and polished view. The coppoer wire has been cut by the bobbin during insertion. Unfortunately, it still Transmitted Energy.

FIGURE 5-4

I hope by now you can predict where this is going. The problem was reported as 8 parts per million that failed. Now you know it is just not so, and the consequences of thinking it is! You now know that the way to approach this safely is to assume that every part is at risk, because they are all exposed to the physics, but only a few cause the ABS system to fail.

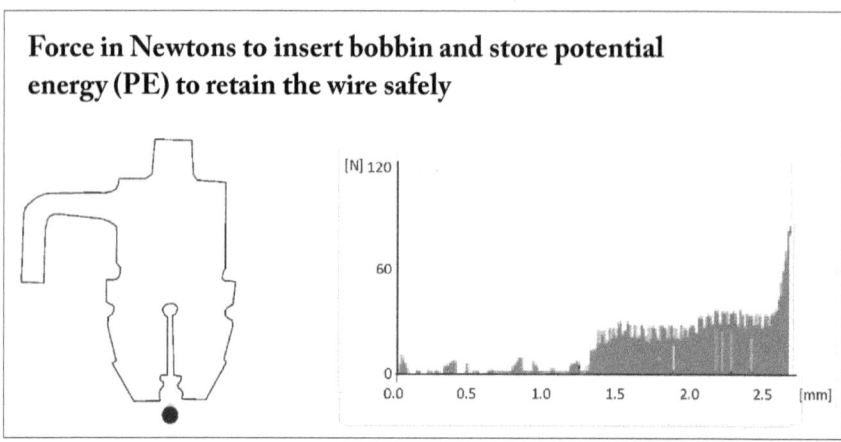

Figure 5-5

The bobbin is pushed down over the wire (black dot) by the linear actuator. Current was logged and converted to Newtons of force. The example above is what we want. The bobbin travels unimpeded over the wire for about 1.4 millimeters, then the effort increases as potential energy is stored to maintain the connection throughout the life of the product.

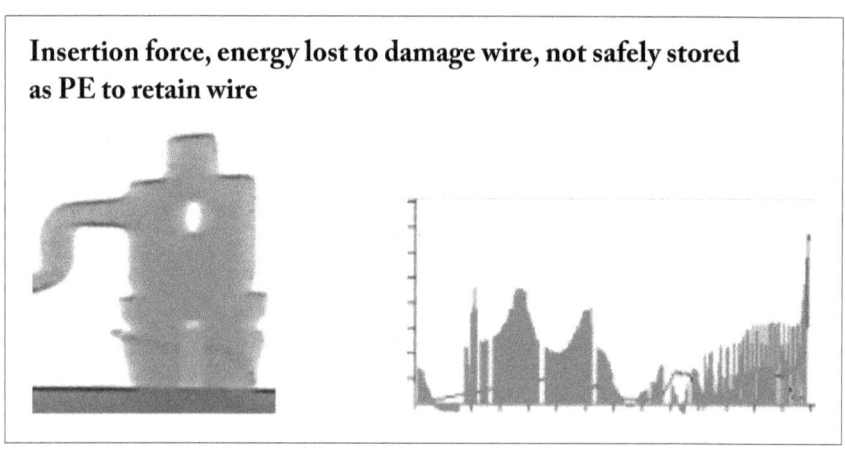

Figure 5-6

In Figure 5-5 the bobbin contacted the wire well before 1.4 millimeters. We know because the current increased too early. It is also apparent that the force was not stored as potential energy, but rather to just cut the wire. This happened whenever the bobbin was loaded at an angle greater than, as I recall, 6 degrees.

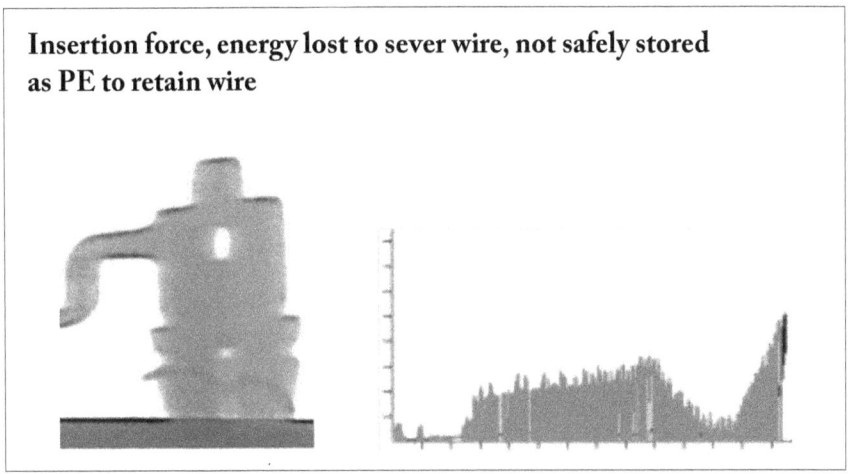

FIGURE 5-7

Figure 5-6 is the most interesting. The wire was not cut, but rather was damaged. It was declared a good part. It was also quite common and easy to find once we knew how to find it. But you already know that now!

The immediate fix was to write a simple program to stop the machine if limits we established for motor-current of the insertion machine were violated within a cycle. Short term: stop the machine and dispose of the part. The better fix was to install a system to make sure the bobbin was placed at less than 3 degrees out of square to the actuator.

Once we were measuring the current to the insertion machine and getting the pictures in Figures 5-4 to 5-6, the story was complete. Perhaps we should have demanded this from the machine supplier and made it part of the validation process.

There are consistent lessons:

- 100 percent inspection is expensive and a poor substitute for characterizing System Behavior.
- Because the insertion machine was flow-based it was easy to monitor, data log, and control.
- Once again, the best and safest approach is to assume every part is at risk. If they are not, the assumption will keep you safe.

The Power of Effort-Flow Workspace

Earlier, we talked about the coating process in the battery plant, which was my first trip with the Gift of Life. We were interested in the coating process, which was described as a long-term *Process Capability* by the quality manager. We now know to characterize the process in order to see the **System Behavior**, which starts with defining a cycle, and decomposing into sub-cycles. We learned to not go beyond two or three serial cycles unless it is called for, as the primary questions are:

- How much of the tolerance is used up in a single cycle?
- Do the second and third cycles look like the first?

Defining a cycle means we have to really understand not only how things work, but also how they work together as a system. We learned that the coating was pumped to a header by a positive displacement screw pump, which is supposed to provide even flow. One revolution of the pump was .6 meters of coated web. In an earlier chapter we plotted the measurement results following Tufte's example of **Small Multiples**.

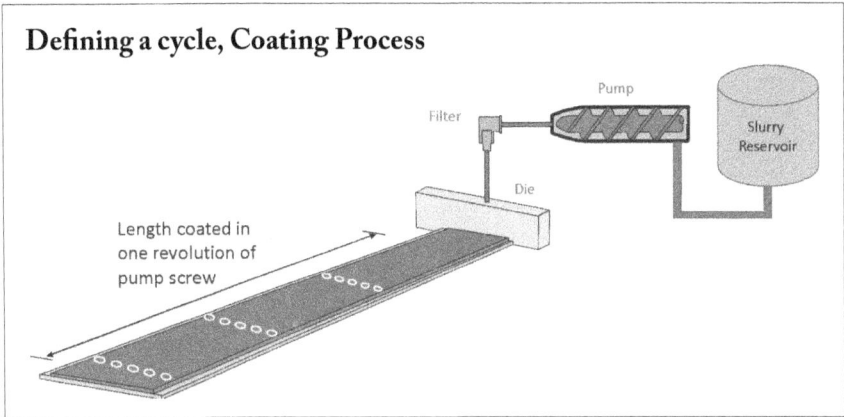

FIGURE 5-8

I had a concern beyond just the coating. The coating machine operator made changes to the pump speed in order to respond to coating weight measured by the tester at the end of the line. He did not make constant changes up or down. The reported values tended to get lower over time, so the response was to increase the pump speed. Now we wanted to have a look at more than three cycles, but still needed a framework. There was a micron filter installed in the pump discharge that had to be changed in intervals that I thought were quite often. The purpose of the filter was to remove fine metal particulate. If it needed frequent changes, I was concerned that it was removing expensive raw material, stripping it from the coating. If metallic fines were causing three filter changes per day, then we would have had another problem! It was far more likely that the filters were stripping out expensive material while changing the dynamics of the pump and coating.

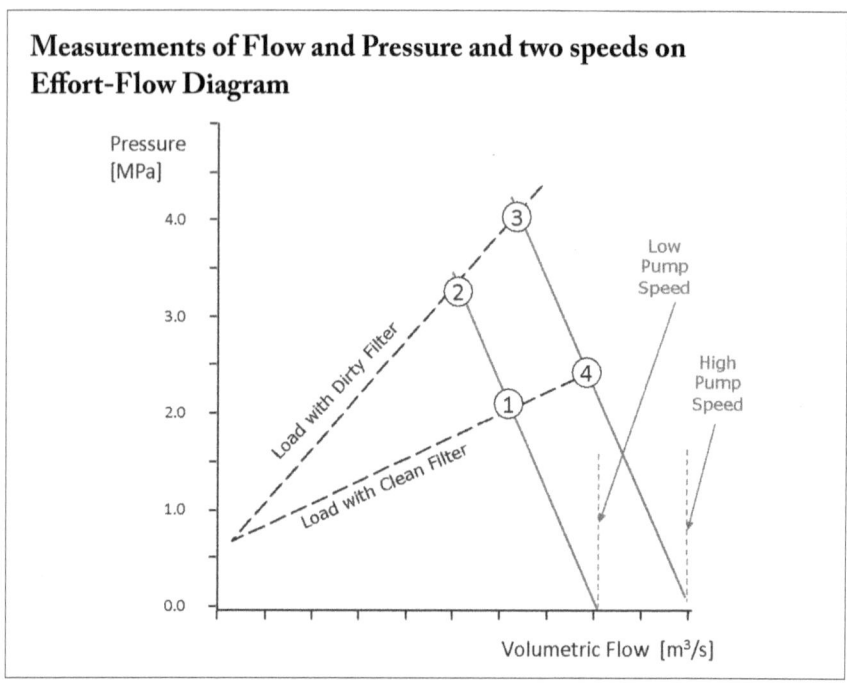

FIGURE 5-9

We learned earlier the power of plotting conjugate variables in the effort-flow workspace. The conjugates for the pump are pressure and volumetric flow. Pressure is the effort variable and always on the vertical axis.

We started with a clean filter at Position 1. The pressure was about 2.0 MPa with a flow rate that corresponds to the position on the horizontal axis. As the filter gets clogged, the pump discharge-pressure climbs from Position 1 to Position 2. The pressure increases to 3.0 MPa, but the flow rate and corresponding coating weight decreases. The operator increases the pump speed, moving to Position 3. The flow rate is back to where it was on Position 1, but the pressure is now at 4.0 MPa. Position 4 results when the filter is changed and the pump speed is not reset right away.

Although the quality characteristic is coating weight, by plotting the conjugates for the pump on the effort-flow (E-F) workspace, we begin to have an in-depth look at what is really happening. Since effort times flow is power, we are left with a question: What are the consequences of doubling the pump power to meet the coating specification?

Characterizing **System Behavior** in the effort-flow workspace provides the ability to ask and answer powerful questions.

- Convergence through a process of elimination is important.
- The full story can not be seen if you look for a Y to X relationship, if what you're interested in is the energetic behavior of machines.
- The story of System Behavior is revealed through paired conjugate variables as power is supplied, converted, transmitted, stored, released and dissipated.
- The effort-flow workspace is a simple graphical representation of the story, which reveals the consequences of effort and flow-based machines.

Anyone who stops learning is old, whether at 20 or 80. Anyone who keeps learning is young.

—Henry Ford

Chapter 6

Expert Knowledge and Dynamic Learning

The last half century has seen the world of quality expand in many directions. There are multiple levels of training. Disciplines have been redefined, split into departments, and renamed. Software has been developed to perform tasks that are expensive while of questionable value, analyzing months of data while the whole story lies in but a moment's worth of easily found information, if we take the time to see with fresh eyes. Competing roadmaps have been developed with this person or that, putting forth an argument as to why you should use 8D (9 if you count the 0) or Plan, Do, Check, Act (PDCA) and Define, Measure, Analyze, Improve, and Control (DMAIC). Of the eight steps in 8D only one has anything to do with figuring out what is wrong, while the other seven are managing problem-solving structure. Six Sigma was applied in hospitals… or was it Lean Six Sigma? Quality is breaking into camps pitting one method against another on social media, where Six Sigma is revered or hated.

There is a new book out claiming to teach Statistical Process Control (SPC) for Operational Excellence (OPEX), clearly a tool masquerading as a strategy, like a hammer looking for a nail. Quality has gone wide, not deep. One might argue that the quality world became its own enemy as it focused on the universality of tools and growing structure, not strategy and innovation.

When I was 15 years old I needed to work. I went to Jack Hackett's Lakeside restaurant in Ipswich, Massachusetts, and asked for a job.

"What can you do?" asked Mr. Hackett.

"I can do anything."

"If you will do anything, then you will do nothing for me."

"I can wash dishes, Mr. Hackett."

I had my first job more than 60 years ago.

"It seems as if we are cheating!"

I don't recall whether it was David or me who said it – but I remember the conversation, although it was 25 or 30 years ago. It doesn't matter who said it first; we were both thinking the same thing. We were breaking the rules and shared the guilt. The conventional approaches to problem solving were not centered on solving problems! While quality makes performance claims in many areas, all we do is characterize and diagnose **System Behavior** to discover explanations for, and to exploit machine behavior. For 30 years, we have gone deeper and deeper, kept our focus narrow, and became the most efficient and effective problem solvers in the world. And we keep it simple while focusing on **First Principles**. By doing one thing, we have dedicated ourselves to learning more and more while remaining dedicated to constraints of effective models and **First Principles**.

Why was the stepper motor project completed quickly? We characterized the **System Behavior** of the product and came to understand it, not controlling a list of variables whether they mattered or not. Once again, I cannot recall ever learning about machine behavior from a list; nor can I ever recall solving a problem based on a list of variables… not once! While others think in terms of lists of things that could go wrong, we approach such problems as a system.

Has Quality Kept Pace?

In 1980, NBC broadcast *If Japan Can, Why Can't We?* Japan had emerged from a devastating war to become an economic powerhouse. American veterans who had only ever bought a Chevy, Ford, or Plymouth were disturbed when their kids parked a Datsun in the driveway. A few years later, the veteran might have replaced his Ford with a Toyota. American manufacturing had fallen behind. Deming laid the blame squarely on the shoulders of management, and credited the Japanese with following his principles.

Deming was generous with his time. I had a few conversations with him and dropped in on his classes at New York University a couple of times. What he taught and wrote was actually quite simple. Deming's most important contribution, in my estimate, was his reference to systems and systems-thinking, be it for how we make things, or a system for profound knowledge.

- "If you only view part of the system, the solutions you come up with can have negative consequences."
- "How you view the system can significantly impact your behavior."
- "Evidence-based thinking isn't as easy as looking at the results. We must have knowledge of the system that provides the ability to understand the results.[1]

Deming had a huge effect on American companies. In the 1980s he drew standing-room-only crowds to his seminars that were, as I recall, three or four days long. Corporate executives competed for his services.

---

1 John Hunter, Deming 101

Deming promoted a system of continuous improvement based on his PDCA[2] cycle. None of it was complicated. In fact, he could get a bit cantankerous with those who asked questions that complicated his simplicity. His message was passionate. He cared deeply, working well into his 90s.

No one, to my knowledge, has been as dedicated to the principles of **System Behavior** as we have. No group of people have worked so hard to develop a simple system to characterize **System Behavior**.

Deming primarily worked alone. He never hired a gang of consultants, but certainly influenced many. He became so popular and in such demand that others saw great opportunity. I was in a meeting in the late 1980s where a well-published consultant was trying to promote his company to a much larger consulting company, taking advantage of his claimed position as a peer of Deming. The senior partner asked, "How leverageable is it?" His primary concern was how to ring the cash register.

Deming got a lot of attention, but never *leveraged* his work. Deming didn't have a brand other than his name and left the door open for others. Others rushed in. Six Sigma became the brand, and Mikel Harry and Bill Smith got the credit. No one owned it, so there were as many versions as there were promoters. Lean was a separate discipline that somehow got absorbed into Six Sigma. One example is a Lean Six Sigma toolkit developed and promoted by ex-McKinsey, Deloitte and BCG Management Consultants, "including all the Frameworks, Best Practices and Templates required to adopt and implement Lean Six Sigma… using the world class *Define, Measure, Analyze, Improve, and Control* (DMAIC) approach. The package includes PowerPoint slides and Excel templates." I think it is fair to say that the promoters were leveraging FOMO, or fear of missing out, and failing to put the proper corporate emphasis on quality.

Six Sigma success, according to Erin Whitestaff of *The Wall Street Journal*, was marginal. "The love affair between American managers and a

---

[2] Plan, Do, Check, Act

wonkish mistress is showing signs of strain, as they fell head over heels for quality improvement programs."

The blame from Six Sigma promoters was certainly not the programs, but rather:

- Lack of senior management involvement
- Cutting short Six Sigma experts' involvement[3]
- Failure to link programs to financial objectives and measure results
- Lack of fit with DMAIC principles
- Failure to launch with a broad scope

After all, Japan was doing it, so why not the rest of us? American consultants became enamored with tools, but not the system. I worked for a Japanese machine tool company many years ago, and in the factory in Japan for a month. If I learned anything at all, it was visual cues and simplicity. The structure never got in the way of the strategy, at least not in the factory.

The Six Sigma gurus were promoting Lean Six Sigma tools, but it was anything but lean. The structure in many companies became massive and dominant. Peter Drucker said, "Mission defines strategy, and strategy defines structure." Has Six Sigma put structure ahead of strategy? I think so, as it copied and promoted parts without understanding the whole system.

Deming never promoted such a quality-centered structure. Deming thought in terms of integrated systems and strategy, not structure and tools. Deming spoke of a system of profound knowledge. Profound knowledge leads to innovation. There is an article I read, but will not quote, that made reference to "Deming's Impact on Six Sigma." Deming had no impact on Six Sigma. But dropping his name might sell.

---

3 This means showing the consultants the door

Dynamic Learning and System Behavior

Our story is simple. It is the story of your experts integrating **Dynamic Learning** *and* **System Behavior**, *because data leads to information, which leads to Knowledge.*

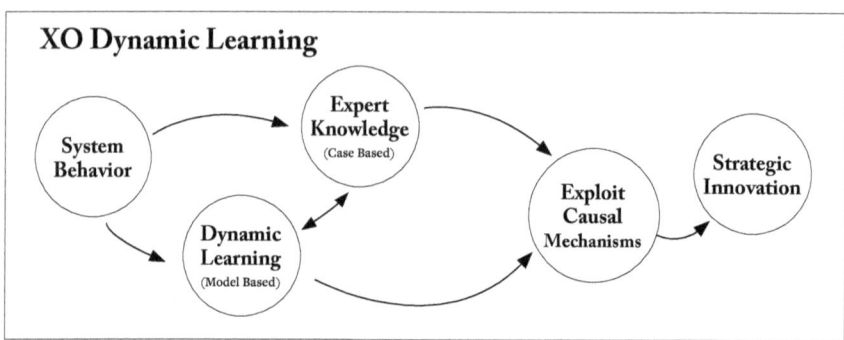

Figure 6-1

The XO Learning Map is as simple as Deming's message. **System Behavior** and **Dynamic Learning** have to be integrated. If structure is defining strategy[4], this simple model will help you fix it without tearing it down.

The foundation of what we do is **System Behavior**. Characterizing **System Behavior** places the emphasis on how the system is supposed to work, and how it is behaving. Such a constraint keeps us away from lists and brainstorming, tools and structure.

This single objective, **System Behavior**, provides insight into

- Performance Engineering
- Reliability Engineering
- Quality Evaluation and
- Diagnosis and Problem Solving

We do not need a separate tool-based approach for each category. **System Behavior** is a simple concept, but what might be the best way to start?

---

4 Strategy and Structure: Chapters in the History of the Industrial Enterprise by Alfred Chandler

I was talking to a trainer a few weeks ago. I like the guy and he is a pretty good problem solver, with lots of certifications and the hats and shirts to prove it. We have done several projects together. He told me he was off to Asia to "teach the tools" in a series of seminars. He will do a good job and people will learn from him. But **Dynamic Learning** is not based on tools. The tools are a function of having adopted a probabilistic Black Box model. **System Behavior** means we are shifting the emphasis to the physical world of how stuff really works. They each have a place. You need to put them together to be the best.

Every **System Behavior** project we have worked on for over 30 years has relied upon some level of expert knowledge. The library of books I have collected over 40 years are stories of **System Behavior**, many of which are told because of catastrophic failures. A few were rather benign, such as claiming the invention of interchangeable parts – certainly important. Others – more interesting to read, some rather painful – drew our attention when steam engines blew up, rockets exploded, and early planes crashed. The *experts* had a lot to learn. An expert might be a PhD who astounds us with brilliance, or a high school graduate who has a few years in a factory with a keen eye, perhaps growing up on a farm working 12 hours a day. We need experts at many levels. Some might earn an hourly wage, while a few have stock options. Every person is not an expert, but every expert has the ability to contribute well beyond what we might expect. Many don't fit the typical structure of a large team and never will. They thrive in a team of two or three, and become lost and fail when a team becomes a committee. Some are annoying, but behind the veneer of annoyance is a level of brilliance that is clear if you take a moment to listen and to see. Think of experts you have worked with over the years. Who are they? Did your organization foster the opportunity for outsized contributions, or were contributions lost in outsized structural impediments?

My library is full of stories about great thinkers who were not experts. Aristotle and Plato were certainly not experts in the way we think of them. Plato and Aristotle are who we think of when making a reference to thought experiments that are important in simplification and application of models. For Plato, thought experiments and inductive reasoning were proof of a concept. Aristotle wrote of deductive reasoning and observation. We can skip over a millennia or so and we come to Galileo and Newton. I argue that neither was an expert, and that such geniuses preceded experts. Galileo was dropping weights from a tower and rolling balls down a ramp during the day, while looking through a telescope at night looking at planets with moons, a contradiction to conventional wisdom. He searched to discover universal principles of falling balls, and moons that were always falling but never hit the planet. Isaac Newton captured the universal governing principle of heavenly bodies ever in motion, and those that fell when dropped from the Tower of Pisa.

How can we put forth that Plato, Aristotle, Galileo, and Newton were not experts? They were not experts – because their role was to discover the principles that were the foundation for practical men and women, the technicians who became experts. They were driven by the need to understand, to see and to capture governing principles. Experts followed, and integrated those principles, which is the definition of **Dynamic Learning**.

We remember Galileo for the questions he asked, and the work he did to gain insight into the principles of the **System Behavior** behind falling and rolling balls. He found that two balls of different mass fell at the same velocity. Aristotle deduced that the heavier ball would fall faster, thinking that logic and reason meant there was no reason for testing with the *base mechanical arts*. The heavier ball, although it fell at the same velocity when Galileo dropped it, contained greater potential energy due to its height and mass, which was converted to kinetic energy as it fell, then released as it hit a wooden pallet. Aristotle was hanging around the conference room while Galileo was climbing towers with balls and mountains with his telescope and his notebook. Experts apply and build on these founding principles every day!

Galileo, Newton, and many others preceded experts. Experts did not discover universal principles such as the Laws of Motion. But with such discoveries by great learners came steam engines, planes, trains, and automobiles, and the experts to make and operate them.

The story of the historical reference to the engineering sciences is based on an understanding of functions, sources, and loads, while learning about behavior, which is how the system responds to inputs and loads. What an amazing story!

The role of experts today is part of the story and the history. However, the scope of experts in the overall scheme of things is becoming narrower each day, while the demands placed on them are increasing. The demand for experts today is like no other time in history. It cannot be done without an understanding of **System Behavior** and Characterization. Systems are more complicated – and where functions and disciplines intersect.

My First Car

When I was a boy, I bought a 1959 Plymouth for $25. I thought it was embarrassing to own a station wagon, so I bought a black sedan with big fins and a blown engine, replacing the engine in the sedan. The list of things I did to that car is long, but I learned quite a bit while almost killing myself before ever getting it out of the garage. Every system was simple. The only electronics, if you can call it that, was a push-button AM radio. I recall that the volume annoyingly faded and buzzed when the windshield wipers cycled while listening to Woo-Woo Ginsberg play the Beatles and the Stones and other songs from the '50s and '60s on WMEX 1510 in Boston.

The technical differences between a 1949, '59, and '69 car were actually quite minimal. All the help and advice I needed came from the guy at the junkyard on US Route 1 in Peabody, or Whitey at Country Motors on Ipswich Road in Topsfield, Massachusetts – which is still there!

A few months ago I took my car in for service in Naples, Florida. I dropped it off on Wednesday morning. The tech in the service area is behind a glass wall. There are no parts to rummage through behind the building. The shop floor is immaculate. I can no longer hang out with a guy like Whitey. It wouldn't do much good anyway. The first thing the tech does is hook up a diagnostic computer. I doubt the guy who hooked up the computer could balance or even change a tire.

Jennifer, the service representative, called a few days later to give me an update. They needed parts and there would be a weeklong delay. My car was five years old. The technology is way out of date. It is ancient! I was given a courtesy car for the weekend. I think the delay was a scheme to get me to buy a new car. It worked. The courtesy car was so amazing it took 15 minutes to get to the point where I could learn enough to safely drive away. I did buy a new car. I was drawn by all the things it does, most of which are still confusing, cool, and useless. A subwoofer under the seats? There are so many cameras, screens, and alarms that it is a challenge to remember to look through the windshield, even though there is a heads-up display. Perhaps they have a seminar.

Experts work in narrow lanes today while the integration of systems is ever more important. Whitey was my go-to guy. He could answer any question about my 1959 Plymouth and he didn't have to Google a thing.

Demands are such that we must learn more and more every single day in order to safely manufacture what was invented only a few short years ago. We all have to keep up! The more sophisticated, the more we must be grounded in fundamentals.

Chapter 6 Expert Knowledge and Dynamic Learning   113

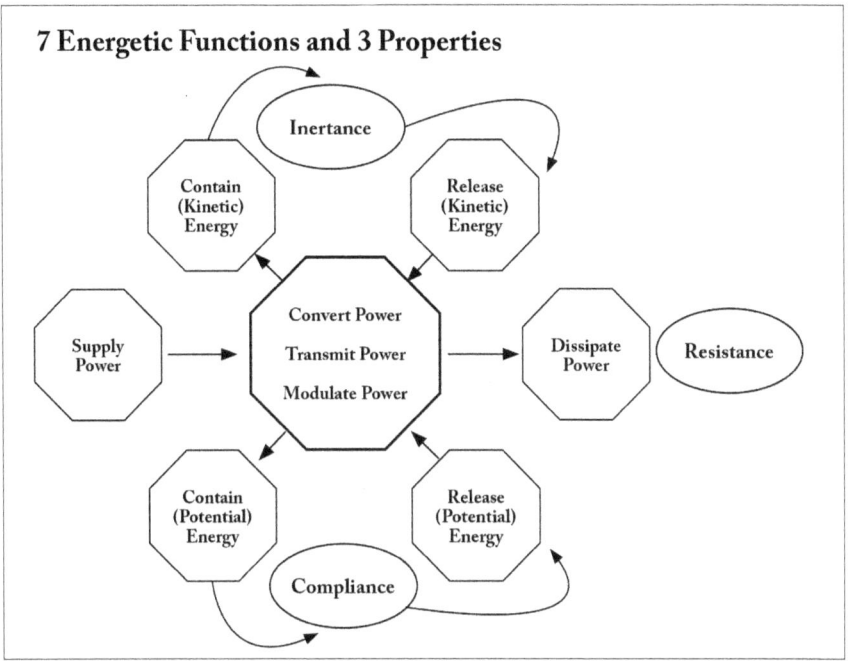

Figure 6-2

Experts have a curious need to know more and more about integrated **System Behavior**. The building blocks are the **Universal Source-Load** model as shown in Figure 1-2 in Chapter 1, and the 7x3 Diagram in Figure 6-2.

Mastering these principles established a perpetual exchange between case-based expertise and model-based **Dynamic Learning**. It is the root of gaining competitive advantage through innovation. Our system, our message, is beautifully logical, and structurally simple.

There is a commitment at a strategic level to develop the ability of experts to contribute more, supported by model-based **Dynamic Learning** while simplifying structure. **XO Dynamic Learning** is a chance to lean-out organizational structure, while giving experts the chance to step outside their lanes – to gain insight and understanding and work together with the people down the hall or in the next cubicle.

The **XO Dynamic Learning** model provides the link from **System Behavior** to innovation, but it will not happen by accident. Leaders who see the power and simplicity of what we have created should think in terms of simplifying the existing structure instead of expanding it.

- Make learning the objective.
- Emphasize Effective Knowledge Capture based on characterizing System Behavior leading to expert system knowledge, not experts in the application of quality tools.
- Replace long and serial-training seminars with project based workshops.

Over the last 20-30 years, many quality departments have become training structures with more and more seminars on tools with less emphasis on project-based learning.

If the objective is really competitive advantage, then Richard Feynman's[5] learning model is worth a look.

- Select a concept to learn.
- Teach it to a child.
- Review and refine your understanding.
- Organize your notes and revisit them regularly.

I have learned more in the last 30 thirty years than I did in the previous 40 by following a model like this without knowing it. David and I selected concepts together based on the desire to learn more about **System Behavior** and what was behind it. Our desire came about because we thought we could do better. I know for certain that by working as a team we did far more than either of us could have done alone.

Select a concept with a fellow learner. Teach it to one another and to yourself. Draw cartoons on a whiteboard as you teach. Simple pictures help us see what is important – and what we don't yet know is important. As

---

[5] Richard Feynman reference

you draw, teach and explain to one another. You are teaching it to yourself as it refines your understanding.

The work David, Tobias, and I have done over the past 30 years centered on interesting projects that we thought had promise. *Diagnosing Performance and Reliability* by David is not just a summary of the project work we have done together. The book centers on what David wrote after we finished many projects and the teams had moved on. We didn't move on. There was more to learn. Learning became our primary interest. We wanted to refine our understanding, to define the governing principles and apply them to new projects. It is why David told the quality manager that we had only been in the rubber business for 15 minutes. It is why I told a manufacturer of oil pipe inspection equipment, "No, I have never seen machines like yours before. But there is nothing you can do with it beyond the functions on the 7x3 diagram."

Organize your notes in an effective way. Then do it again. As I write this, I have notebooks, reference material, and loose papers with notes I scribbled in my office as well as at the dining room table. They are not as organized as I would like. It takes too long to find what I need. If I were younger I would learn how to take electronic notes and develop a filing system. David is the best notetaker I have ever met. If I call him about something we did together years ago, he has it at his fingertips.

Most training departments follow a project roadmap where the emphasis is on project summaries demonstrating the ability to apply certain tools in the course of completing a project. Once again, there is no need to change much. Just look at each project for opportunities to learn, and a way to organize a system of learning, which is bigger than each project.

I suppose we might call it a System of Profound Knowledge.

"The tendencies that emerge from probabilism are complexity and uncertainty...

*In physics, we find an astoundingly
"improbable" interpretation of probabilism...*

*As Bertrand Russell states,
"probabilism is the antithesis of law!"*

*Probabalism states that something is true because it works.
Determinism states that something works because it is true.*

—Walter Babin, Determinism vs. Probabalism in Physics

Chapter 7

The Black Box Trap

Knowledge and application of the Black Box model and **Sparsity of Effects** principles are fundamental to the quality, product performance, and reliability professions – so are the limitations. George Box said, "All models are wrong. Some are useful." Box has a permanent and deserved place on the Mount Rushmore of statisticians. Box is quoted by nearly every trainer who teaches designed experiments, which are based on the Black Box, but few seem to realize his statement was a warning. I doubt that Box could ever have imagined the degree to which his warning would be ignored and how important it is today.

An Interesting Definition

In science, computing, and engineering, a black box is a device, system, or object that produces information without revealing any information about its internal workings. The explanations for its conclusions remain opaque or 'black.[1]

That is a warning we must heed. Furthermore, the Black Box treats scientific theory simply as a formalism or a mere device for delivering predictions from data. We need to know what the inner workings are and to look inside the Black Box.

---

1 I lifted this from a source I can no longer find.

The Truth Is *Inside* the Black Box!

Not long ago someone asked me what I thought of Artificial Intelligence (AI). I was reluctant to answer but said, "I think of AI about the same as nuclear energy. It has the power to do great things as well as to destroy." AI is the ultimate Black Box model. AI can be used to analyze huge databases while the conclusions remain opaque if the inputs pass through the Black Box. With today's computing power it is easy to abuse if we accept the opacity without question. If we accept and understand the limitations, we can better utilize its power.

AI can do great things in many fields, but we need to be aware of the consequences of writing algorithms to get around or even ignore physical law. That is where the warning from George Box applies. The Black Box model is powerful and important, but we have to apply it responsibly. Buying a software package that makes it easy to run experiments does not alleviate your responsibility to know the risks. The risks are often lost in beautiful graphics and lots of statistical analysis that might be better if simply plotted on a whiteboard by hand. Make machines do the tedious work, never the thinking.

Chapter 7 The Black Box Trap

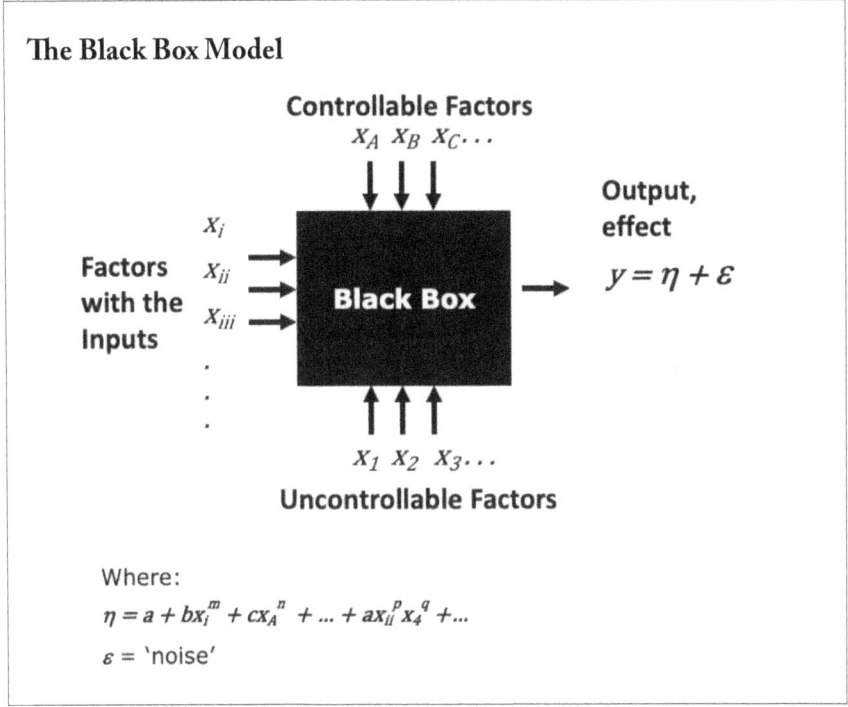

Figure 7-1

The summary model is as interesting as it is simple:

$$\eta = a + bx_i^m + cx_A^n + ... + ax_{ii}^p x_4^q + ...$$

Equation 7-A

It merely states that an output Y can be computed based on Xs as independent variables, as well as how they interact with one another. Figure 7-1 shows three categories of Xs: those that are controllable (maybe with knobs and dials), Xs that come as inputs (such as raw materials), and lastly, those that are theoretically uncontrollable (such as humidity, which everyone likes to blame for all their problems). The summary equation means that we can use it to represent just about anything we want without knowing what happens inside the Black Box. The summary equation above could also be reduced to:

A = P + R

Equation 7-B

It simply means that all the observed variation, A, is split into two categories: the part that was tested, P, plus the rest, R. It is important to keep this in mind, as the objective of any progressive search is to strategically apply the **Sparsity of Effects** principle to avoid the mental complexity of *All these variables*. **Sparsity of Effects**, properly applied, means you can often split the Black Box into two groups and eliminate one without listing variables at all!

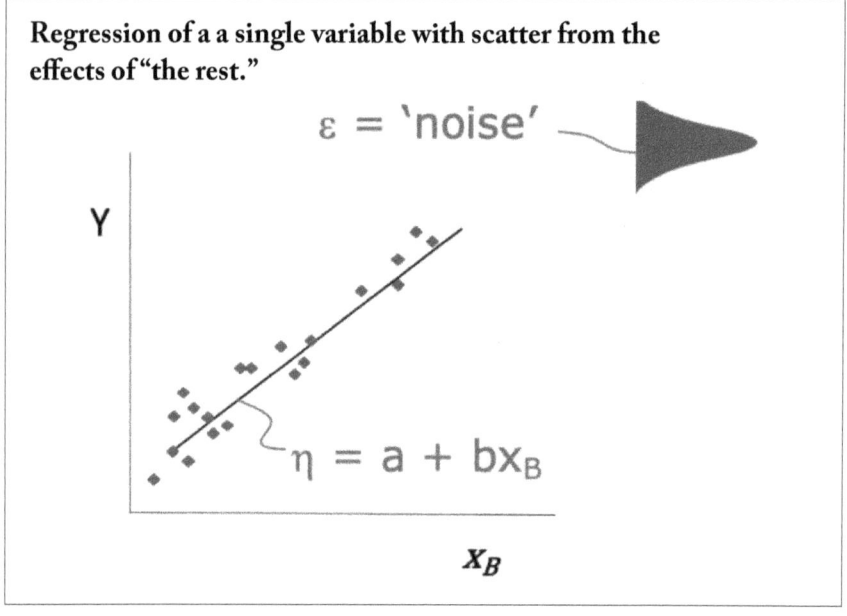

FIGURE 7-2

Figure 7-2 shows a regression analysis of a variable, X_B, where:

$$\eta = a + bx_B$$

Equation 7-C

The Y-axis can be divided into the part that is from the variable X_B on the horizontal axis, and all the other factors, which Figure 7-1 shows, are divided into three categories. The rest of X variables are given the chance to influence the output, but not manipulated in the course testing and controlling X_B. The *noise*, or vertical scatter, is the effect of all variables other than X_B. To read this, we might say that X_B is quite powerful because it has the ability to affect Y with minimal interference from the rest of the variables. The equation 8-C merits one more look: the "b" in front of the X in the summary equation represents the slope. The slope of any and all of the three groups of input variables shown in Figure 7-1 could be calculated if we were so interested. We can lump each of the three groups, if we so choose, but not the X_B. If we lumped almost all of them – if the process were properly designed and controlled – they would have a slope near 0. They would be called *Flat Xs* since the output Y hardly responds to changes from that X. In other words, as long as the process limits are properly established, the window in which the three groups of input variables from Figure 7-1 drift around is small enough so that the output, Y, does not appreciably respond. In theory, the larger the window in which each X can vary, the better off we are as long as the slope remains flat.

Although A = P + R can divide variables into two groups, the Part in which we are interested versus the Rest misses over the power of **Sparsity of Effects** in this case. Why test one single variable against all the rest when you can simply split the Black Box into two groups – if you know how – and eliminate large blocks of variables without ever naming them?

When I first was exposed to the Black Box, I thought "that's interesting," but I became wary. I knew the model had value; but I saw too many flawed applications wherein the Black Box was skipped over. There were those who were enamored by the software and skipped over the thinking. In several cases where it was abused, the limits for the X on the axis created a steeper slope than was realistic because the boundary limits were too tight – or the sampling plan did not give the rest of the variables the chance to show their true influence.

"How can you replace **First Principles** of science with a probabilistic model?" I wondered. Thirty years ago, I did not know that George Box was warning us. The Black Box model is no substitute for understanding **System Behavior**.

There are just two strategic approaches to looking inside the Box, which are described in the previous chapters. They are,

- The Source-Load-Impedance model
- **Matryoshka-Small Multiples**

These two strategic models give us a chance to shine a bright light into the Black Box. Whenever we are asked to work on a machine performance problem, be it the machines you bolt to the manufacturing floor or the machines you make to sell to your customers, these two models are the basis for changing the question from "What is wrong?" to "What is happening?" The first question may yield a steep but questionable slope of an X claimed as the root cause. The second, based on asking "What's happening?," would yield a **Causal Explanation** of **System Behavior** inside the Black Box.

Where to start? The truth often lies in the dynamics of but a moment; but the moment has to be properly selected and observed to reveal the truth. The moment of observation is where dynamic learning takes place. To ask "What is happening?" means to ask "What is happening *right now*?! How are machines behaving at this very moment?" There is no need, as we have learned, to wait around for defects. If you have made any, just assume everything you make is at risk until you prove they are not! And never wait around to collect a bunch of data and *then* do an analysis! When the idea is to find out what is happening right now, it follows that we expect to learn one thing… today!

The **Source-Load** model is a way to really see with fresh eyes. The output of a machine is not a single Y; it is energy conjugates decomposed in an E-FAST diagram and plotted on the effort-flow workspace. This allows us to have a new and insightful look at **System Behavior**.

Those two simple and powerful strategies are the starting point for any and every diagnostic investigation into **Systems Behavior** *and performance and reliability engineering.*

Matryoshka-Small Multiples and **Source-Load**, properly applied, crack open the Black Box. When we heed George Box's warning, we are careful so we can conduct designed experiments on a limited but more meaningful and powerful basis. We do this to prove we know what we are talking about instead of running huge experiments to search out some steep X. We can control what needs to be controlled and really understand it without wasting resources on what does not matter.

Looking inside the Black Box is precisely what has provided scientists, engineers, and technicians the ability to learn, the source of centuries of innovation, creating the machines that make our lives what they are today.

Let's look back on the anode-coating project. There was a mountain of data, collected over an extended period, that had been analyzed six ways to breakfast. A report calculated all the statistics you could possibly want. We could project the results onto a screen in a PowerPoint summary for a Teams meeting around the world. People might ask if the variation was common cause or special cause, or ask about short-term and long-term capability. Someone might put up a fishbone diagram, an annoying *tool* that has no relationship whatsoever to the physical world, and no place in true diagnostics.

A short walk to the line with a notebook and pencil to draw a cartoon of a cycle or two, followed by a collection of a couple of meters of material to measure and plot with **Small Multiples**, provides far more insight than months of statistics where the truth was averaged away.

Just as we can waste mental energy in life, we can do the same thing while problem solving. Many of the projects we have worked on around the world were because people were working on the wrong things. They thought it was important to make sure every possible reason for variation was identified and addressed. Deming said, "All *systems* must be stable." He never said you have to control every variable. Looking at the smallest effective differences in the span of a single cycle is where the truth begins to reveal its nature.

Sparsity of Effects – Few Things Really Matter

In life, there are principles and constraints that keep our minds focused on what matters. Without such constraints, we would look back and think of all the things we worked on and yet how little we accomplished. The ability of humans to accomplish great things is extraordinary. I have learned over the years that extraordinary people have the ability to know what to work on – not wasting energy on the trivial. If David, Tobias, and I know what to work on, it is not because it is innate in our soul, but rather because we taught ourselves, one another, and many of you.

In the work we all do, **Sparsity of Effects**, if understood, adopted, and practiced as a founding principle, will help you become an extraordinary engineering and technical problem solver. **Sparsity of Effects** is a founding principle, not just an interesting quote for a PowerPoint presentation.

When we are called to help solve a tough problem, we often find the people working on a project confused and frustrated. They are not having any fun at all. No fun is a dead giveaway that the strategy is flawed. No fun, combined with Zoom or Team calls two or three times a day, and you have entered Limbo, Dante's first circle of hell.

Symmetry

There is a beauty of symmetry in the physical world that we seek to exploit when we characterize **System Behavior**. When we take that important step to ask, "What is happening right now?," we are opening our eyes to see the beauty of Symmetry in **Systems Behavior**, with the next step: drawing a cartoon.

Drawing a cartoon provides a model-based topographic map that allows us to see inside the Black Box, to capture machine action as it creates a geometric form or energetic interdependencies of the system, be it a manufactured part, an energetic response, or both.

In *The Character of Physical Law*[2], Feynman tells a story that begins with examples of **First Principles** and their discovery. (His books are easy to read because he is such a great storyteller.) He describes the nature of Symmetry in geometric forms like spheres and polygons. He quotes German mathematician Professor Hermann Weyl, who defined symmetry: "a thing is symmetrical if there is something you can do to it so that after you have finished doing it, it looks the same as it did before."

Cartooning and **Matryoshka** are both the development of a plan to capture the symmetry of a system. **Small Multiples** is the graphical representation of what we see.

Feynman goes on to say, "The laws of physics are symmetrical; that there are things we can do to the physical laws, or to our way of representing the physical laws, which makes no difference and leaves everything unchanged in its effects."

---

[2] The Character of Physical Law, Richard Feynman, 1965

That is what we are trying to capture; but you will miss it every time if your model of probabilism steps over the Black Box.

Twenty-five years ago I was driving from Detroit to my home in New Hampshire, listening to National Public Radio. While crossing the Hudson River on the Tappan Zee Bridge in New York, with only a few hours to go, I was listening to an interview with a nuclear physicist. While describing the behavior of subatomic particles, he said: they were not fully understood, and that, unfortunately, probabilistic models had to be applied. He went on to say that one day, the principles will be understood and thus able to describe such behavior with a physical law as opposed to a probabilistic model. He also said that the **First Principles** description would be simple. I found a rest stop and made a couple of notes. Why, I thought, were we applying Black Box models to problem solving when the **First Principles** are understood? Why did we default to a probabilistic view based on large sample sizes when **System Behavior** can be described with **Source-Load** and **Matryoshka-Small Multiples** with a sample size of just one?

Power of Probabilism

I have to take drugs twice a day so my transplanted heart does not reject. The drugs lower the ability of my immune system to fight off infection. The first four years after transplant, I was taking one particular anti-rejection medicine. One of the side effects was microscopic tears in the smallest of the blood vessels in my new heart. The tears are a precursor of rejection. Whenever you have flow in a pipe or a vessel, molecules of the fluid attach to the sidewalls, whether the flow is turbulent or laminar. In my case, the blood cells, not native to the heart, didn't like being there and pushed their way through the blood vessel wall, creating a microscopic tear. The way researchers figure this out is to look for DNA in the blood that is from the donated heart. The more foreign DNA, the greater the damage and the associated risks, an indication of rejection. I was prescribed a new drug to solve one problem, but it had its own side effects.

"John, research indicates that this has about an 80 percent chance of working," the doctor said.

"That's good enough. It will work for me."

"With that attitude and thinking, I suspect it will."

What other choice did I have? It has been three years with the new drug and I am doing well. A recent test result said the new drug is working with 97.5 percent confidence. I am not quite sure what that means, but I like it! There is no physical law that I know of that describes this behavior; but the doctor described the fundamentals of how it worked.

The analysis of these medicines and side effects has to cover a wide variety of patients and patient conditions. They do not work perfectly for everyone. For some, it might not work at all; and for a very few, the results might be catastrophic. In order to get approval for such drugs, they have to be tested across large sample sizes. The results have to be carefully analyzed, with risks uncovered, and if they are unacceptable the drugs cannot be used.

The reason I needed a heart transplant was because my heart was damaged as a result of a rare reaction to a drug that is a blood thinner. My blood was clotted, not thinned, and I had a massive heart attack that nearly took my life. It was the luck of the draw. I understand that. Life expectancy is not deterministic. There is no physical law that governs such behavior.

I am alive because of the research that has been done since the first heart transplant in 1967 by Dr. Christian Barnard in South Africa. The recipient died soon after from pneumonia. When he died, his new heart was working. I was 17 years old when this was in the news. Little did I imagine that the probabilistic research that was happening at that time would someday save my life. By the late 1970s, heart recipients were living about five years. In September 2024, I celebrated seven years with the Gift of Life, and I look forward to many more.

The people who saved my life at Advent Health in Orlando, Florida, are brilliant. They know and understand and contribute to the research and advancements. They also know there are risks – and so do I. They cannot state with any certainty what the relationships are between the drugs I have to take and the outcome. They rely on probabilistic analysis, and rely on improving the outcome for most, knowing it does not work the same in each case.

This is not to say that medical research is done in a Black Box. Research is conducted knowing the strength of effects and likely outcomes. But they keep working to find better and better ways to save lives like mine. The analysis might be Black Box, but the researchers strive to carefully gain insight into what is really happening.

As I told my cardiologist, Dr. Raval, "What we do in our field is easy in comparison." **System Behavior** starts with an eye toward governing principles that are deterministic by their very nature. **System Behavior** is simple in comparison to human responses to medicine and environment.

As I write this in Naples, Florida, there is a tropical storm between Cuba and the Florida Keys headed up the Gulf of Mexico. I have been switching the TV from the Olympics to the Weather Channel for the last several days, keeping an eye on Hurricane Debbie. The brilliant experts on the Weather Channel tell the probabilistic story of potential hurricane development with proper warning as to what might happen. Two years ago, Hurricane Ian was predicted to go well north of here. Ian was said to have a 90 percent chance of making landfall near Tampa Bay. Against all odds, Ian took a hard right turn at the last moment, slamming into Fort Myers, just 30 miles north of Naples. It was devastating. Of course, there were those who blamed the weatherman. Forecasting the weather will always be uncertain, but the expert knowledge gets better and better with each event. Those of us who make things have it much easier.

Many of us were taught the Black Box model, to think in terms of variables, Xs – and how changing the levels of Xs influence the output, a

Y response. The flaw is that we overlook what is happening inside the box! The technical aspects of what is happening in the Box cannot be replaced with a probabilistic explanation.

Now you know how to see inside the Black Box and when to use it properly. I hope that we have done a fair job of the same while limiting our scope to **System Behavior**.

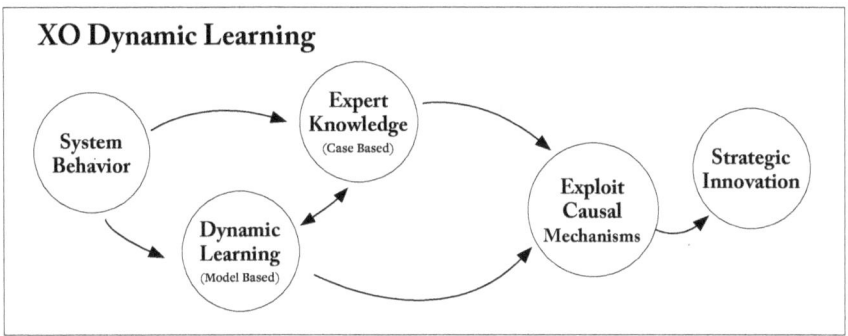

Figure 7-3

Black Box, Sparsity of Effects, and Progressive Search

When I decided to write this book I thought I would just be able to share 30 years of experience and finish in a couple of months. That was delusional. David, Tobias, and I are closing in on 100 years of shared experience. Amazing! Even with so much to draw from, it was not enough to meet the objectives we had established:

We want to change the world of Diagnosing Performance and Reliability engineering, to set a new standard for effective model-based problem solving, while showing how simple it really is.

To change the world, experience told through stories alone was not enough. It was important to effectively demonstrate that what we do is based on not only years of experience but also grounded in good science and research. One of the most fundamental elements is a Progressive Search while learning more each day.

The concept of a Progressive Search is centuries old. The objective is to eliminate the improbable and the impossible and be left with the truth. The idea is simple enough, but the starting strategy determines if it works. Our approach, characterizing **System Behavior**, is to take advantage of the physical constraints of products and processes to conduct such a search effectively.

There is a distinct advantage of conducting a progressive search based on how the physical world reveals its nature. The beauty and symmetry of geometric shapes and **First Principles** guide us to **Source-Load** and **Matryoshka-Small Multiples**. We start small, often with a single cycle, and never have to talk of variables, but rather the groups in which variables are connected. The Black Box model in Figure 7-1 divides variables into three groups, which has little diagnostic leverage.

A fishbone diagram attempts to divide a response, or the fish head, into bones of a skeleton into categories that have no diagnostic or practical value whatsoever. There are several references that claim *a fishbone diagram is a cause and effect discovery tool to help reach consensus for reasons for defects, variations, or failures within a process, and to break it down into potential root causes.*

That is not even responsible, nor is it diagnostic.

Figure 7-2 divides the world into A = P + R. The response tests a single X variable against all the others, or R.

The first call we received from the lithium battery manufacturing company was because the coating was coming off the electrodes, and being returned by customers. The response was the decay in power output of the battery, which was one reason the team thought it would take a long time to figure out – or to find the *root cause*.

They had run a series of Black Box-designed experiments and thought they had reported improvements. They were smart enough to know it might have been something of an illusion.

It bears repeating that the team members I first met in Boston were brilliant; however, they did make something of a mistake at the starting point. They defined the problem as *coating delamination* and ran a series of experiments based on Black Box, of course, to try to improve the slurry and coating process. Search as they might, the results were *inconclusive*.

Actually, they were conclusive – they just didn't like them. Let's remind ourselves of the equation:

$$A = P + R$$

The results of the tests indicated the problem was in the R, or everything other than what they were testing.

They had defined the problem as poor adhesion. All the experiments were designed to improve the coating adhesion based on slurry mixing and composition. The team made an assumption when they defined the problem as one of adhesion. We restated the starting point to *Coating Comes Off*. This is much different – and not a conclusion but merely an observation. They might have been working on the wrong thing based on an assumption that might not be true. If the adhesion were fine, but there was some subsequent event that knocked the coating off, it could be represented as follow:

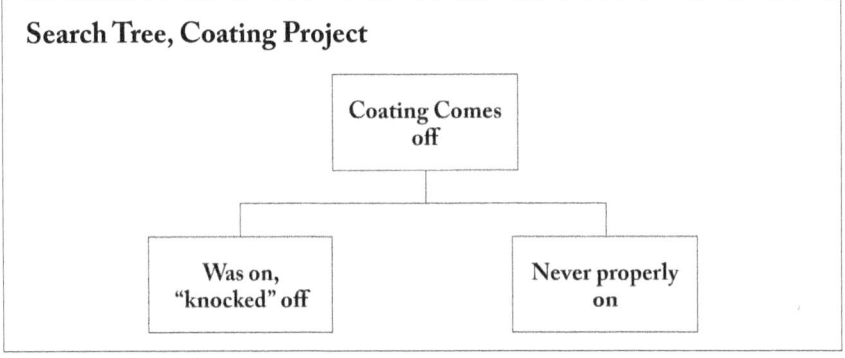

Figure 7-4

The statement in Figure 7-4 is simple and powerful. It includes every single variable as one alternative or the other without naming a single variable. The statement takes advantage of how the manufacturing system is organized in serial steps.

In order to figure out which statement was true, we would need to find some indication, or precursor of failure, in the finished product before it was shipped, and that was not decayed in battery performance.

Only a few batteries were selected for disassembly just before they were ready to be shipped. They had not been in the warehouse for long – but we got a clue. I also found out why no one wanted anything to do with disassembly. Lithium is highly volatile and flammable as well as dangerous to smell.

FIGURE 7-5

There was a consistent and uniform pattern in that the coating began to flake off at the top. The top was established at the pouch loading station. There was no *top* until the anode was sliced and trimmed well after coating. The pattern was not visible in field returns, as the decay pattern was destroyed. This begs the question, "If we flip a few of these and insert them into the pouch so the *top*, as shown, becomes the *bottom*, will the pattern follow the part or remain with the process?"

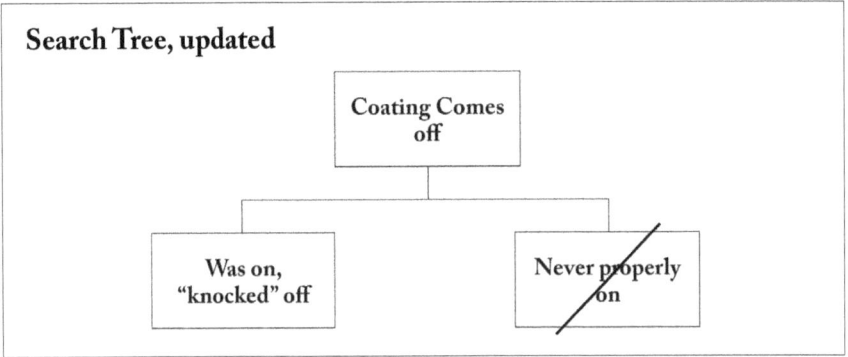

FIGURE 7-6

The assumption that the coating adhesion needed to be improved was shown to be defeated by the power of an effect that was outside the coating process, or in the R. Once we got this far, the brilliant minds on the team knew right where to look. A designed experiment was run, not to explore the effects of a group of variables but to confirm that the physics were correct, and that the effects of the proposed solution were in the P in the equation, $A = P + R$.

There are two sides to this story. First, how did such brilliant people get fooled? Because they had developed the coating science! They had put so much effort into constantly improving adhesion over the years that it was difficult to conceive of another possibility. They struggled to believe the results of their own testing, because it was outside their belief system. (Perhaps the influence of those doing the analysis influenced them as well.) Every person I know, including me, has fallen into the same trap.

"

> *Using standard statistical methods is like driving a car at night on a poorly lit highway to keep from going in a ditch. We could build an elaborate system of bumpers and guard rails and equip the car with lane departure warnings and sophisticated navigation systems and even then we could at best only drive to a few destinations. Or we could turn the headlights on!*[3]
>
> **—Aubrey Clayton**

Clayton goes on to claim, "Science, statistics and philosophy need one another now as much as ever." I completely agree! The science comes first and statistics keep us from driving into the ditch.

If the statistics keep us from driving into the ditch, how can we turn on the headlights?

Sparsity of Effects

Those of us who work in characterizing **System Behavior** have a distinct advantage over medical researchers, or philosophical and economic statisticians. The work we do is generally right in front of us, and rarely needs data collection over long periods of time – but rather, right now, begins with a single cycle. Probability of a failure mode might be important to *analysis of warrantee*, but characterizing failed functions with **Source-Load** is where the science takes over.

---

3 *Bernoulli's Fallacy*, Aubrey Clayton, 2021

Brainstorming variables, fishbone diagrams, and exploratory designed experiments are a clarion call to take a new and fresh look at the foundation of Diagnosing Performance and Reliability.

The **Sparsity of Effects** principle is why A = P + R even works in an effective progressive search.

"We have 25 percent failure on a leak test when we use part A, and 40 percent when we use part B. We need to figure out what is different."

Actually, you don't. It will consume a lot of time and resources to try to figure it out, and the answer will be unsatisfactory. We know that when a certain percentage passes while others fail, none are really any good.

"We have a 5 percent difference in performance between Line 1 and Line 2, but each has a high reject-rate. We need to figure out what is different."

Such a waste of time! Why not just choose the worst machine, characterize **System Behavior**, figure out what is happening right now, and, for the moment, ignore the difference between machines? You can figure out the difference later. **Sparsity of Effects** will likely be obvious by then.

The ability to sort out the noise in the midst of a catastrophe and focus on what really matters is what sets apart the best problem solvers from those who are average. As Taylor Swift said, "I am intimidated by the fear of being average." She certainly isn't average and has the discipline to be extraordinary.

If you look up the **Sparsity of Effects** principle, you would find: *In statistical experimental design, only a few factors, usually main effects and lower order interactions, are statistically significant while the majority of the others have no effect on the outcome. This principle highlights the idea that experimental resources can be used more efficiently by focusing on the important factors rather than investigating all possible factors.*

Even if the definition is correct, it doesn't help strategically for characterizing **System Behavior** when diagnosing performance and reliability. Few things really do matter. The question is: *How do we figure out what matters quickly?* How do we avoid running experiments, which are generally expensive, and avoid missing the truth, which often lives in the Rest? The truth often ends up a surprise, and would not show up on any list of variables.

Equation 8-A shows that individual and interacting Xs add as variances, or squared values. Not only is it true that few factors matter, but also, since the total observed variation is a function of the square of the individuals, the ones that matter will readily reveal themselves if you know how to ask proper questions to find them. The model,

$$A = P + R$$

helps us take advantage of the definition. The squared power of variables means not only that they show up if we know how to find them, but also, if we are working where they are not, we will get miserably confused. The "coating comes off" team was trying to figure out how to improve coating adhesion. They were working in the R, or the Rest. The truth was in the P, or the Part they weren't aware of.

Suppose they really do make an improvement. Would we see it in A?

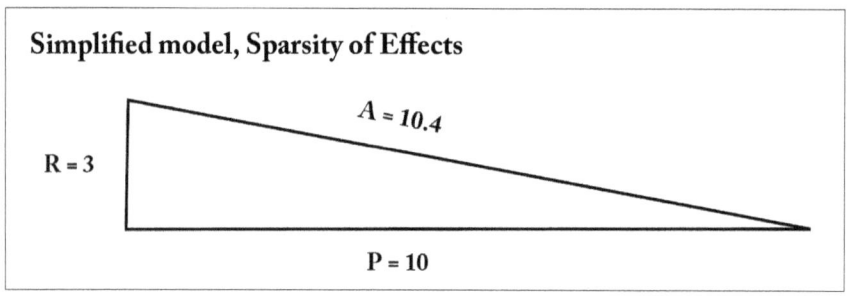

FIGURE 7-7

If R is reduced from 3 to 1, a substantial improvement, what would happen to A?

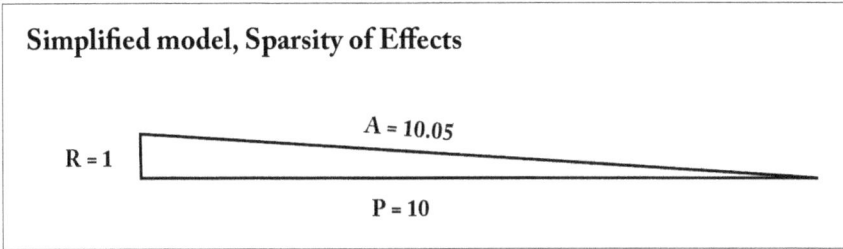

Figure 7-8

Reducing R by two-thirds has virtually no observable effect on A. Do we run more experiments with variables you know the name of, or do we back up and realize that the truth and the real power, lies in the Part missed over?

That is precisely what we did with the simple isolation test for the coating project. The problem was not that the coating was coming off, but rather that it was being knocked off as a result of a process change (no, I can't say what it was) well past the coating operation.

Reducing the biggest effect, which was in the part not being tested, is the only way to have meaningful results.

David, Tobias, and I have trained ourselves and one another to see what matters and not get lost in what does not. Our starting point is **System Behavior** grounded in **First Principles**, changing the question to one that works, while forcing a product or process to reveal its nature. It took a while to recognize **System Behavior** as the starting point; but now it is the basis for everything we do. It really does keep things simple.

Don't ever begin with a list of variables. Characterize System Behavior and give the truth a chance to reveal its nature. The truth is System Behavior, and it lives inside the Black Box.

Truth, like gold, is to be obtained not by its growth, but by washing away from it all that is not gold.

—Leo Tolstoy

Chapter 8

Structural Decomposition

Structural decomposition can be helpful to narrow down the scope of a problem, but it is never a replacement for characterizing **System Behavior**.

Sometimes, in an effort to dogmatize a model, the essence of the model is damaged, which gives credence to *"all models are wrong."* One cannot overemphasize the importance of thinking in terms of models and the limits of models. Models, if universally and broadly applied, can lose their power. Keep the applications limited. Trust the simplicity of effective models.

Often people want a roadmap of some sort. We have one. Tobias was the driving force in putting it together. I resisted, I suppose, until I saw what he had done. He kept it simple and efficient without making it a rulebook, leaving room for creativity.

The starting point, *Establish the System Scope* and *Create the Starting Question*, are quicker and more effective than a problem definition. These two steps draw a virtual fence around the problem, a mental application of A = P + R.

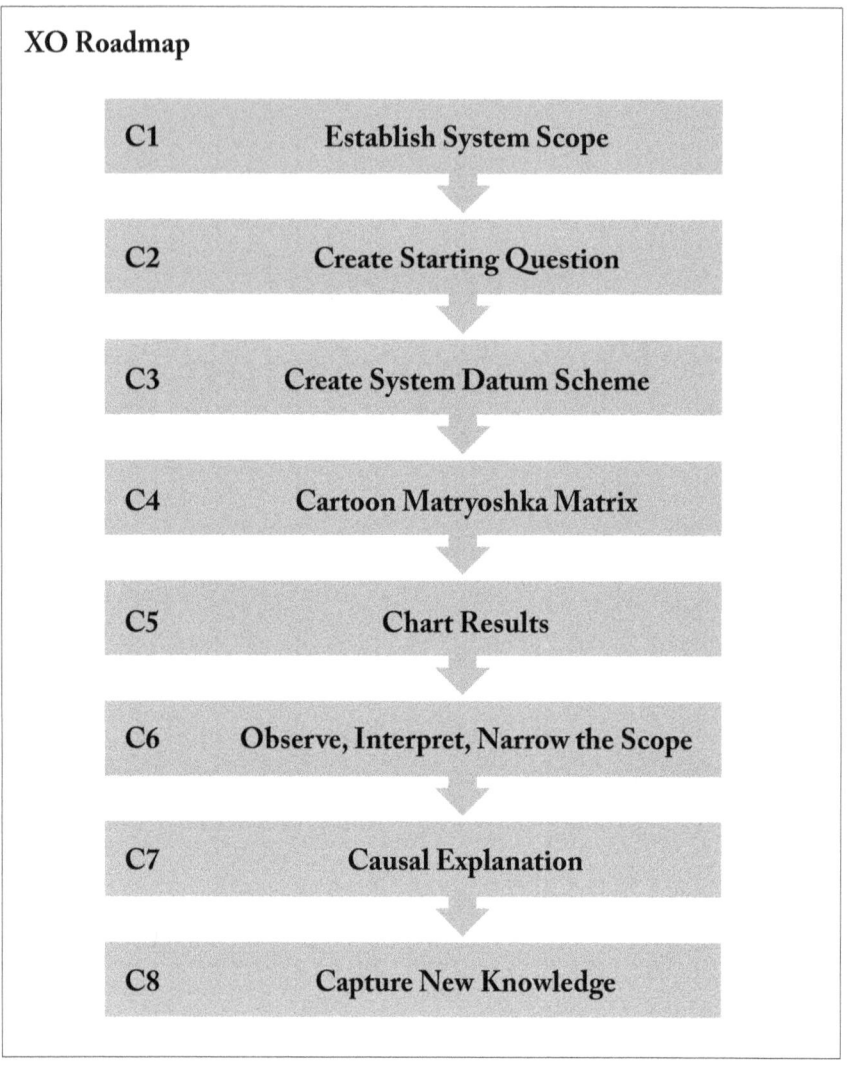

Figure 8-1

Roadmaps imply a universal approach and what tools to use. There are no tools at all on the XO Roadmap. Just like the map application on my iPhone, there are alternate routes based on *what is happening* on the roads.

Running a factory might call for standard work. The science of characterizing **System Behavior** calls for an adherence to **First Principles**, represented by *Functional Determinism* and the creativity of integrating **Expert Knowledge** with **Dynamic Learning**. **First Principles** provide a powerful constraint. I often hear, "We need to think out of the box." I have no idea what that means, how to do it, or where it leads. My reply is, "We need to stay inside the box defined by the nature and laws of physics and how characterizing **System Behavior** will reveal that nature."

The fundamental strategic approach is based on starting with the proper question, once again, because that is how science is done. We also know the importance of changing the question, and thus the strategy, when called for. "I don't know" is not a failure when the question is "What's wrong?" as long as we change the question to "What's happening?" and characterize **System Behavior** with the strategies we have been learning, beginning with **Source-Load** and **Matryoshka**.

The Limits of Structural Decomposition

Once in a while, as a subset of "What's happening?," we might find structural decomposition as a way to speed up the search and narrow the scope. Structural decomposition is a way to get an answer to the question "What is different?" based on what things are made of when different behavior is captured. There is no path to a **Causal Explanation** directly from structural decomposition. Structural decomposition can help with a Progressive Search to quickly narrow down the scope of a problem, but it only helps to see what is different!

A full **Causal Explanation** calls for an answer to "What is Happening?" That means that structural decomposition, which centers on looking for differences – generally when swapping parts around – is limited as a standalone strategy because it cannot tell the entire story. It is also probabilistic. It may get us closer; but a **Causal Explanation** must, with rare exceptions, be deterministic. I recently watched an online presentation where the conclusion was that a five-factor interaction caused an annoying mechanical noise, discovered, the presenter claimed, by swapping parts around.1 This flies in the face of the **Sparsity of Effects** definition. A five-factor interaction is a probabilistic pipe dream for a simple mechanical noise. I don't know how the presentation ended. I clicked out.

The statement "Everything you need to know lives in the difference between the best and worst" is flawed. The difference can help, but "everything you need to know" is just not so. As we improve our manufacturing capabilities today, it becomes even more important to question this statement. The days of large variation in manufacturing variables are closing. In every project I have described so far, we have found that the answers are deeper in the physics of what is happening. You are blocked from the truth if you believe that what you need to know solely lives in differences.

LCD Display

A company asked us to work on a project for Liquid Crystal Display (LCD) speedometers that were failing in vehicles. Every number from 0 to 9 can be represented by a blocked array of seven LCD lines. All the display lines are black and visible for the digit 8, and two aligned vertical lines are visible for the digit 1. A failure is when any are missing. For example, you would read a 0 if the middle horizontal line is missing from the 8.

Whenever any device in an automobile fails, the costs can be breathtaking, especially if hidden deeply inside the instrument panel. The stepper motor sold for $1. It cost $1,200 to replace. The cost associated with diagnosis, and that borne by the supplier, can be backbreaking. The bent and leaky brake line project was expensive and caused recalls. The ABS coil

---

1 *Process Quality Control*, Ellis Ott, published in 1975, is a good source for the study of variability in manufacturing before it became dogmatic. Ellis introduces **Analysis of Means** in Chapter 11 with decision limits for a single mean value. Current approaches use limits for two means. I like this book. Ellis knew his way around a factory.

failure cost was staggering, and we know that all of the damaged parts were not found. By the time we get involved with any of these projects, the stress and pressure to figure out the problem is painful as the costs pile up fast. Fear on the part of the managers is translated to panic and anxiety on the part of those doing the work. These are times when characterizing **System Behavior** is called for because swapping parts around has already taken too long without gaining new knowledge. If they had only said "I don't know what is wrong, but I have a way to figure it out" a bit sooner!

Imagine the look on the face of the senior manager when we say, "Our job is not to solve the problem. It is to learn at least one thing every day about the physics of function and failed function." They had been trying to solve the LCD problem for weeks and had not figured it out; so why would we keep doing the same thing? Characterizing **System Behavior** is about learning – which can be fun, if you let it. I think every person who shows up for work should be able to go home at night and feel as if the company is better off because he or she came to work that day. This is important. For many years, I have been telling myself and the people we work with that our job is not to solve the problem. I do it because it is important to make progress every day, to be constrained effectively, and to keep from mentally wandering around *out of the box*. Model-based learning sets us up for daily progress. If you have been working on a project for days or weeks without learning, you are facing failure. I might also argue that your time has been stolen. If nothing else, we want to show you how to learn fast and love it! I can *teach* you effective strategy; but what we really want is to *show* you that this is in our soul.

On the LCD project, we were told there were no failures at final testing. "We have 100 percent good parts at the end of the line test." That's not accurate nor is it even helpful. If this is what you believe, then you have trapped yourself in a broken model. All the parts pass inspection – but that does not tell you how well they work. The mistake they made was to assume that passing inspection meant the parts were good. Since structural decomposition calls for pairing good with bad when you swap parts around, the team mated a reported failure from the field with a so-called good one and got confused.

Structural decomposition is not functional or deterministic. It assumes there is some structural difference in part geometry or a property that drives the difference. It may be structural, but inefficient in any event. Look at Figure 8-2.

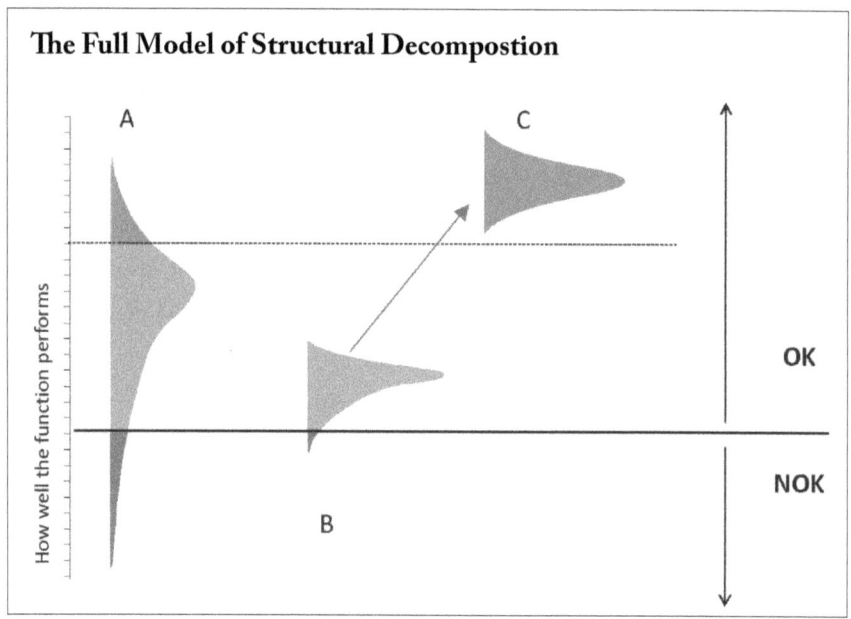

FIGURE 8-2

- If A is true, you have a good chance to find the good versus bad difference structurally.
- If B is true, and you assume A, *structural decomposition* will likely fail.
- If A is true and you assume B, *functional decomposition* will succeed.

The objective is to make B like C. Asking "What is different?" won't get you there. I recently drew this on the whiteboard while meeting with a senior vice president of engineering at a company that manufactured steering systems. He said, "We don't make junk like A, and we have been better than that for 30 years." But they were still swapping things around because *using the tools* became the strategy.

Tools and roadmaps can be impediments to **Dynamic Learning**. If you really want to excel, then integrate models and guidelines into your thinking and drop the dogma of tools and rules.

I wrote in the introduction that I wanted to tell a story. The story would not be complete without telling how David, Tobias, and I evolved and grew by challenging the conventional wisdom. We have challenged ourselves and made mistakes. Our mistakes may have centered on a failure to tell our story in a simple way. Initially, we talked about the details of discovery. The details were important for discovery and learning – then to learn how to communicate the lessons simply. The details might have been important to us, but we became a bit too enamored with them, knowing that what we had done was extraordinary. This put us in a rush to tell everyone. I suppose that might have been our fate, because revolutions can be painful. Even within our own organization there were struggles. But we have stayed together for half our lives, becoming great friends and building something that is powerful – and at the end of the day, simple.

It was certainly over 20 years ago when we rented a training center outside Detroit to teach a seminar on the great things we thought we had done. The people who came knew us well and expected a lot from us. We let them down. Our message was not simple or clear enough; but a few said that what we were doing was special and to keep at it. Al Dickenson, no longer with us, was a good man and a brilliant engineer. Al spent a lot of time with me to help work on the message. We were solving tough problems and doing it fast – impressing people – but our story was weak. We just were not at the point where we could tell people *why* it was that what we were doing was so powerful – especially those who were structurally invested in tools and dogma. We certainly did not give them enough of a reason to change the game. But they did keep bringing us back to solve tough problems, often pairing us with one or two people who became quite like us. Judson Estes, Gordon Brown, David Horne, Xiangji Bu, and Paul Mackalski and his team are just a few.

As I look back on the story of quality improvement since the 1940s, I feel it is fair to say that no three people have pushed themselves so far, or for as long, as we have. We have evolved and grown.

I think what we are most pleased with is that we have challenged ourselves, learned more, and developed the models by which we live, all while making them more powerful and simple since the seminar in Detroit years ago. And we did it as friends.

After weeks of frustration and failure, we figured out the problem with the LCD in a couple of days once we changed the question to "What is happening?" and characterized **System Behavior**. It is a simple change to make to provide pride of workmanship to your problem solvers, and a competitive advantage to your company through innovative solutions with the integration of **Expert Knowledge** and **Dynamic Learning**. And frankly, it is fun.

Figure 8-3 shows a circuit board with the copper conductors, an elastomeric zebra strip, and an etched glass LCD cell. The board logic determined which LCD segments to energize, or de-energize, based on vehicle velocity. The function of the zebra strip is to *transmit power*. The zebra strip was quite interesting. If you look closely, you will see black and white stacked layers. The black layers are conductors and the white are insulators. The idea is to have six or seven conductors to each copper strip on the board with several white insulators between each copper conductor, thus making sure the proper LCD segment is energized.

Chapter 8 Structural Decomposition   147

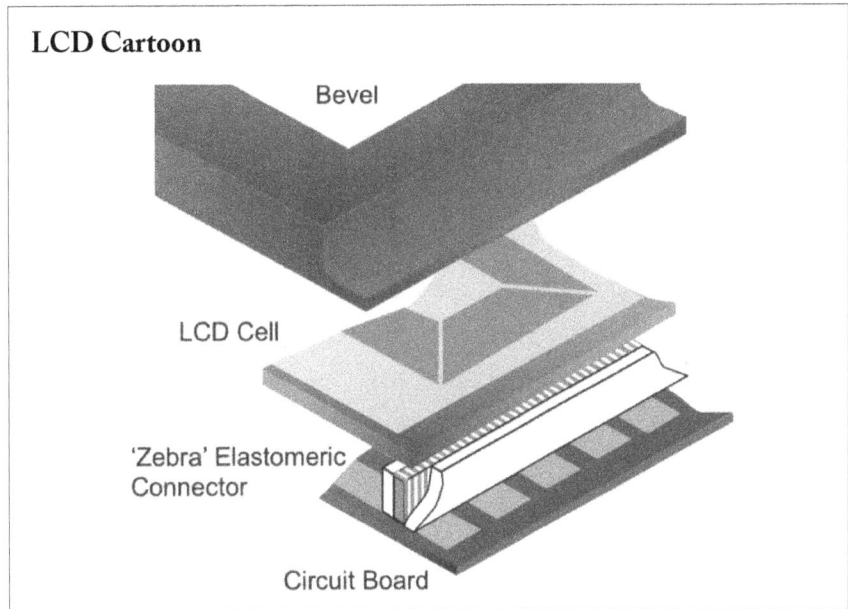

FIGURE 8-3

The problem is that if we get a field failure and take it apart and put it back together, it works. Actually, it *worked* before they took it apart, but not well enough. The logic wanted to see a clean square wave, not a messy one. They were all messy, but some messier. There are two possibilities in the conventional wisdom of component search: *Parts* or *Assembly Process*. If the difference is preserved, it means the problem lies in the parts. If the difference is not preserved, it does not mean the difference is from the way the parts were assembled. The logic only works in one direction. If the fault lies in logic based on code, which it often is today, swapping things around will only get you confused.

The team had checked the resistance from the etched glass, across the elastomer to the copper trace on the board, and thought it to be okay. This is important. Checking resistance might reveal if you have a complete circuit. It is never the full story of the function. We are interested in the ability to transmit power. There are countless examples over the years of problem solvers getting confused when looking at half of a conjugate pair or an alias variable. I used a few mechanical examples for leaks and fittings; but the same logic holds in electrical transmission. Characterizing **System Behavior** and a bit of discipline goes a long way toward avoiding confusion.

I was suspicious of the zebra strip, but that was based on our knowledge that Transmit Power is a function that typically merits a look. There was a clue that I didn't think was given enough consideration, which was that the LCD segments that failed were often powered through the very ends of the zebra strip. Once again, checking resistance was no help.

There was a clever guy in the test lab. I asked him if we could hook up a capacitor to discharge through the circuit to get a picture on an oscilloscope of the transmit power function. A capacitor is a small device that contains and releases a charge. It has some of the same properties as a battery.

"How big of a charge do you want for the capacitor?" he asked.

"I don't know. I don't want to burn anything up. I just want a picture on a scope that lets us see what happens as the charge is released and passes through the zebra strip."

He opened a drawer and fished around. "One of these oughta work!" I love that approach.

In short order we had the test results shown in Figure 8-4. New ones looked like the expected signal. I then sprayed some silicone onto the glass section of the LCD that was smooth. The assembly process squeezed the zebra strip to keep it in place. With the spray, the zebra strip quickly spread out, but only on the end that contacted the glass. It did not slip where it contacted the copper, which kept it from slipping.

Chapter 8 Structural Decomposition 149

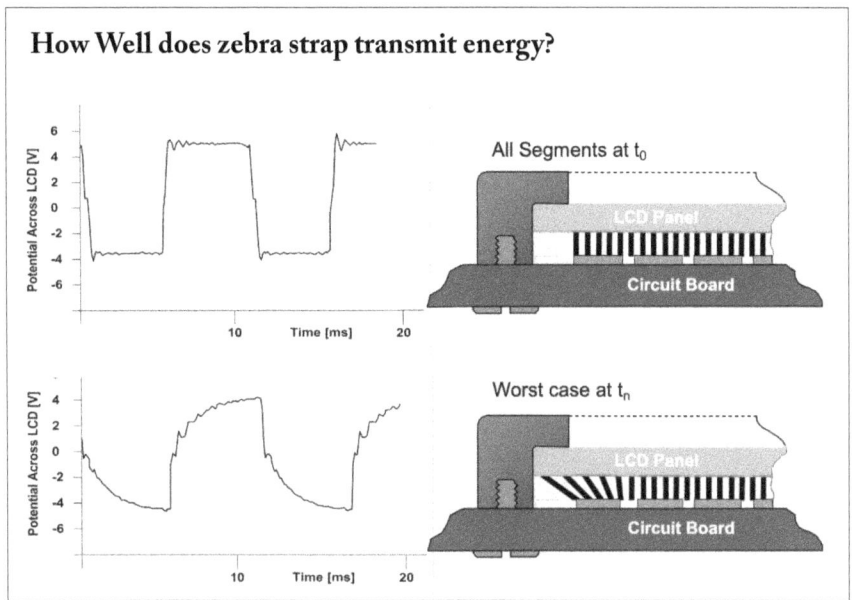

Figure 8-4

Once the zebra strip slipped, or crept, as it did over time in the field, there were still one or two conductors across from the glass to the copper, but not the six or seven needed to provide a clean signal. The losses in transmission as the zebra strip creeped over time increased, causing the failure. A wider strip that did not creep was purchased for the same cost. Were there really good and bad parts? No. All of them were at risk.

The truth was, once again, that every single one was at risk.

Condition B in Figure 8-2 (page 144) was true. Often people ask, "What is wrong and what tool should we use?" They begin by assuming Condition A, and look for good and bad parts to swap around to try to find a difference. They get confused because the model is flawed. All they need to do is to change the question to "What is happening?" It really is that simple.

It is essential to say: "'I do not know." This is precisely the attitude of the truly learned man, who is always launching out into areas that are beyond the limits of his knowledge.

—**Francois Michelin**

Chapter 9

Models in Life

All problem solving starts by asking, "What's wrong?" Problem solving should start that way, reading the Symptoms, hopefully by people who have a level of expertise sufficient to solve the problem at hand.

If asking "What's wrong?" leads to confusion, big teams, action items. and frustration, then we need to change the strategy. Remember, the question drives the strategy, so change the question! Once the strategy is changed, make the objective **Dynamic Learning.**

"What's wrong?" vs. "What's happening?"

David wrote that on a whiteboard one snowy day a long time ago in Cirencester, England, to start off a discussion of how different actions would follow each other, given that questions dictate strategy.

I loved the trips to England, where we worked to figure out the principles of what we were really doing. We never once tried to create tools, then find a place to use them. Instead, we tried to put some order and discipline into the process of forcing products and processes to reveal their nature based on **First Principles**. These are the physical laws under which they are designed – and govern how they operate while learning and seeing with fresh eyes.

Being a lover of history, as is David, I liked where he lived in medieval Cirencester, especially when we left the office and went around the corner to Black Jack Street, a narrow alley with cute shops that had replaced metal working and foundries of years gone by. Legend has it that there was a statue of St. John the Baptist on the church tower at the end of the street. The smoke from the furnaces blackened the statue to such a degree that the statue was called Black Jack, to the offense of a few and the delight of good-humored Englishmen. At some point that became the name of the street. Keith's Coffee became my favorite place… or was it the paper goods store where I liked to buy notebooks and cards, both on Black Jack Street. David liked showing me the remnants of the Romans as we walked around the park. It is interesting how each story of history helped us learn to see our own way.

Changing the question from "What's wrong?" to "What's happening?" was a simple but brilliant breakthrough. Actually, we had changed the question many years prior when we thought we were cheating. But it was in Cirencester, near Black Jack Street, when we came to build the **Analytic Logic Map** that is on the cover of David's book, *Diagnosing Performance and Reliability*. A simpler version has evolved into the **XO Dynamic Learning** model.

Such places always set my senses on fire, helping me to see and feel the history of creativity and innovation – not bound and restricted by rules and tools, but rather learning from those who have gone before us.

Now we know that characterizing **System Behavior** is the objective, and that it takes a combination of expert knowledge and a sound model-based learning system, which, we know as students of history, is the only path to innovation!

I started this chapter by writing that all problem solving starts with the question "What's wrong?" I wrote that sentence, then leaned back in my chair and folded my arms. Should I write what I am thinking? Is it too personal? Would the personal story help make a link to the world in which we work? I leaned forward and decided to take the risk. Heck, I thought, most who know me already think I am half crazy. I know I am, and I am fine with it.

Even in life, when we have a problem, we ask, "What's wrong?" Sometimes, there is no answer and life can become miserable or even desperate. There was a point in my life where I was miserable. The story took place over several years, perhaps 2002 to 2006. What happened is not as important as how I reacted as it happened, why I think it had to happen, and where my life went as a result.

I thought long and hard about telling this part of the story of my life. It is too personal, I thought, and I am the only person ever to have lived who has experienced such things. Nonsense. I am older now – and every older person knows that no life worth living has been without challenges and difficulties. The best of us figure out how to survive. The real story is how we center our lives on models that give us the help we need to get through the difficulties of life – especially when merely asking "What is wrong?" is not working, but we keep on doing the same thing! We like to joke that the definition of insanity is doing the same thing over and over while expecting different results. In life, it is no joke. Desperation comes from trying to figure out what is wrong, knowing no other way, leading to bitter loneliness and worse, while staring into the abyss of who knows what. Then comes the day when those of us who learned much of what we know about manhood in the military – models based on ships of wood and men of steel – have to find the courage to ask for help.

In the early 2000s, how I defined myself fell apart. I did not like where I was working, and it had become so intertwined with my life that I felt trapped. My actions were less than helpful. As a result, I lost my identity and more. Or so I thought. I had not a single moment of peace – but did not know it. I just knew I was miserable and living in mental torment – trouble sleeping, waking up exhausted, unable to focus on anything. I wanted to be around people, but just couldn't. In what I thought was a total repudiation of manhood, I went to a psychologist for help. At one level, I hope you think this is funny. On the other hand, this nonsense held me back. My silly models, ingrained over a lifetime, were literally killing me.

I wish then I had known that something was wrong with my heart. I thought my dizziness and nearly passing out were because of my mental state. To the degree they were intertwined, I have no idea; but I lived for years with a heart problem. David knew my speech patterns were impaired and getting worse, and we talked about it. I thought it was early Alzheimer's. Later, I found that it was because I was not getting enough oxygen to my brain. I needed help!

I made a good patient for the psychologist – but not at first. I was defensive, giving reasons for everything about why I was right. I was lucky she put up with me. At some point things changed. I began to see that the only thing she could do for me was to help me change my mind – to change the model when asking, "What is wrong?" It worked, for the most part. I took a lot of notes, and wrote about what I was learning, and about the evolution of my thoughts.

I decided to sell my beautiful condo in downtown Portsmouth, New Hampshire, which has since tripled in value. I then bought a blue water sailboat, which I would sell years later for about a third of what I bought it for. My life was an adventure. When not on the boat, I was either working with people like you or wandering alone in some jungle or city meeting people not like me – learning from every adventure and every person. Sometimes I look back on that period, wondering if there was a simpler way. Perhaps not for me. Perhaps the adventure saved my life. I was writing stories about what I saw as I traveled in jungles, sailed on the open sea, rode trains across Europe, and I posted them on a blog. I had two blogs – one about work and the other about my adventures.

One story was about building a new model for life, one that worked for me when asking the question "What's wrong?" failed. I wrote that story because so many people I met fascinated me. The goal in life, they claimed, was happiness. That seems like a good idea on the surface. However, some, if they did not seem happy, swung between a level of euphoria and sadness, then sought answers in self-help books. With those experiences, and the notes from the psychologist, I started to write the story. I wrote it about the same time David and I were developing the **Analytic Logic Map** that integrated **Dynamic Learning** with **Expert Knowledge**. I suppose it had to happen that way: one changed how we did characterized **System Behavior**, and the other, how I lived.

I thought I knew periods of happiness. Perhaps happiness is fleeting. Perhaps the nights of sailing the ocean under the Milky Way with smooth seas and a following wind were perfect moments of ideal peace. Maybe we seek happiness, but should rather accept the treasure of perfect moments rather than happiness – perfect moments such as when a child is born, or we see a beautiful sunset, or even the sense of learning from a good teacher or teaching a good student, or learning ourselves – perhaps even when completing a complex project.

The story turned out to be quite simple. I was struggling at a personal level. I found I was failing at trying to figure out what was wrong. I was wasting energy. Working and wandering the world, I met men, women, and children who really did have little, but were smiling. I wasn't. When I had the awful feeling that I was not happy and knew of no alternative to happiness, I was at a loss as to what to do. I had to learn to ask different questions – the key to learning.

The first question was, "Am I at peace?" Certainly not. At the worst of times, I had to learn to change what was in my mind's eye – to see with fresh eyes. The psychologist in Portsmouth taught me that in order to do so, no matter the time of day or night, I had to walk to the Piscataqua River. It was not far from my condo. I always found peace as the tide from the ocean I loved flooded Great Bay, then drained again hours later, pulled by the moon. That it happened for thousands of years before me, and would continue for thousands of years after I was gone, seemed to put my life in perspective. I learned what to do to find peace because the walk to the river, no matter how cold, changed what was in my mind's eye. I had to learn to clear out the thoughts that took over my mind. It now applies in everything I do. I was living the life Mark Twain described when he said, "I have suffered a great many catastrophes in life, none of which has ever happened."

Peace can only be found in life and in the work we do. We need to keep the model in mind that most things do not matter – that the **Sparsity of Effects** principle applies to life as well as characterizing **System Behavior**. Finding what does matter is the secret to a good life as well as being a superior problem solver. Neither will happen without a system for learning.

Living in peace led to a life of living in harmony with those around me, as well as gratitude for each day. For the most part, this is simple for me now. Living with a heart transplant makes every day a gift. I also put a lot of effort into keeping my life simple in every way.

I sometimes wonder if the most difficult thing I ever did was to learn to keep my life simple.

This is the model I learned for myself – just for me. The point of this story is the consciousness of having a model fail when you ask, "What is wrong?" I wonder to this day about the timing of what I learned. My heart, I suspected, was failing; but when I sought a diagnosis, the reply was, no trouble found!

I was in Tampa, Florida, on my way back to the airport in October 2016, with a car full of supplies for Ariadne, my sailboat docked near the Panama Canal, ready to sail across the Pacific. My life got quite simple in but a moment when I passed out while driving at 70 miles per hour on my way to the airport in Tampa. A month later, I woke up from a coma in Orlando, skinny and barely alive. My family had been told I would likely not survive 48 hours. Once I came out of the coma, I was told that survival meant a heart transplant. I knew that life was not promised; new hearts don't come from Amazon. I also knew that for me to live, a healthy person had to die. The very idea was difficult for me. My life was worth no more than any other. I knew that I had to do my best to live a good life, to be a good man in order to merit the Gift of Life. While in the hospital I had an image of a good man at home with his wife and kids, whom he loved, who would lose his life in an accident and save mine. The only way around it is to live well in his honor. Most organ recipients feel the same.

As I look back, I cannot believe my good fortune. I was rarely in the USA, other than to work or change flights in Atlanta on the way to Europe or Asia, as my boat was in the Caribbean. I have been down the stretch of road near the Tampa airport many times since that day in October. I passed out in heavy traffic because my heart valve had failed. I did not hit another car – it happened in one of the only places without concrete barriers that might have killed or maimed me or others. I could have passed out at sea, on an airplane, in a jungle, or on a remote island. I don't believe it was just luck. I had surgery in a hospital in Tampa, where I was given a drug that I was allergic to that gave me a massive widow-maker heart attack. I was airlifted while in a coma and on life support to Advent Hospital in Orlando, where my life was saved.

I never once asked how long I would have to wait for a heart. Others died in that year of me waiting in and around the hospital. I had to come to grips with my life as it was – and possibly death. I never complained, because I knew what it would do to my soul. I was really living life on life's terms, however short it might be. It was a model that worked for me.

```
V = 120v  →  ┌─────────┐  E = 100
             │Transmit │  →
I = 1A       │ Power   │  I
             └────┬────┘
                V-E│ I
                   ↓
```

```
V = 120 Volts
I = 1 Amp
E = 100 Volts
20V x 1A = Dissipated Power
```

Most of the things I had thought were important before October 2016 seemed to fade in importance. My life had come down to one simple thing while waiting for a heart… stay alive one more day! Every day when I woke up was a gift. I would look out the window and see the sun (or rain) even though my mobility was limited to the length of hoses and wires to the machines keeping me alive. I was at peace.

Staying alive one more day became my mental model. When all you want is to stay alive, life has a way of becoming simple – but only if you let it. I think it's a guiding model that lets you ask for help. My sailboat had been my home and was in an anchorage near the Panama Canal. So what? How much would it cost to be in the hospital month after month? Who cares? I might not get out of here anyway! My life as a sailor was over. Where would I go? It could be down the street or the far side of the moon; it didn't matter. What mattered was to stay alive… one more day!

I needed help. I was not from Florida. My nearest family was my sister, Lucille, in Alabama. My nearest friend was Elaine in Tampa. I spent a lot of time alone, which often means you spend too much time inside a dangerous place – your own mind. I learned to ask for help, although it still put my sense of manhood at risk. My son brought a guitar. The hospital got a teacher for me. Elaine brought food, a break from hospital food… and ice cream! Lucille came often and took me out to eat – early on in a wheelchair. I had calls every day from Antonieta, my wonderful friend in Panama. I still have the stack of cards I received from so many people! They are important to me.

After weeks in a coma and a bit of recovery, I was moved to another hospital to get stronger. I could not walk and was far too sick to get a new heart. I was alone, in a small room with a hideous paint color and a single small window. A woman came to get me. Her name was Zamarys Roman. With the help of two others I was lifted into a wheelchair. My life had been about living outside. I had been fit, could climb the mast of a sailboat, could raise and tend the sails at sea, and do all the work that had to be done while in an anchorage or dockside. Zamarys wheeled me outside – the first time the sun had touched me in weeks. As the sun kissed my face, I began to weep. I was skinny, having lost over 30 pounds, sick, and unable to walk. I looked dreadful. Zamarys stopped the wheelchair as I cried, putting her hand on my left shoulder, giving me comfort – a man she had met as a patient merely moments prior. As her hand rested on my shoulder I thought of how close to death I had come. Sam, my son, and Barbara, my ex-wife, were at the hospital during the weeks I was in a coma. They were told I would likely be dead before long. Twice, I had to be brought back from cardiac arrest. But here I was! Zamarys, for some reason, took a special interest in me. I was soon out of the wheelchair. She took me to Disney World while I was still attached to machines. Now, at least once a year we have lunch in Orlando. She brings her beautiful daughter, born since she first helped me. Six years after receiving the Gift of Life I visited her family in San Juan, Puerto Rico. She really touched my heart – opening her kind heart to me.

When healthy enough, I was moved back to Advent Hospital in Orlando. I was asked by those saving my life what they could do to help me, which they did each day. I replied, "Help me maintain my mental, physical, and spiritual strength." It took a team of three people just to get me up for a walk. It took forever to make a few trips around the ward, as I wanted to stop in every other room to see my new friends, many also waiting for the Gift of Life, some not surviving the journey.

Maintaining my mental, physical, and spiritual well-being as I lived just one more day became my model, my guide for simplicity, and subsequently my model for life. As life goes on and I am further from receiving the Gift of Life, I suppose I have to admit that there are times when I need to do a better job of practicing the model that was so hard to learn. I do know that I have to keep my life simple. That will never change.

Everyone has a model for life. Some are useful and a power for good and well-being. Some you choose for yourself. Some are passed on to you from generation to generation. Some are a function of your environment and culture. Some are destructive. Some are useless. Some open your mind, while others close it off. All are powerful. Some are based on empathy and the ability to see the good in others. What guides your life? Does your life guide your work? Does your work help others? I am aware and I try. Some days I fail; most days please me. But I know to compare my days to the models that guide my life and work.

I know one thing for certain about models. If they are not simple, they are useless.

I suppose that if I look back on more than seven decades of life I could characterize it as a perpetual search for simplicity, concentrated in the last two decades. I can now quickly sense complexity and do what I can to steer clear. This holds true in both my personal and professional life. Perhaps the search for simplicity, while constrained by principles, transcends both.

In every endeavor we undertake, I think peace comes from finding simplicity. I take several dance lessons a week and have been doing so since about a year after I received the Gift of Life, a new heart. I started because it is a wonderful way to meet people, and more fun than going to the gym. Dancing is a way to find peace, in that it takes concentration on the task at hand as well as exercise. You cannot learn to dance while wondering about anything else. Your mind's eye must be clear. The people at Crossover tease me good-naturedly about my dancing. Little do they know that it really is part of my search for peace. Then again, maybe they do know.

Barbara Chacon, my Bolivian teacher, has made her life teaching people to dance. She emphasizes the beauty and simplicity of dance, and how much less energy it takes when done properly. "For this move, the axis of rotation is me, not you, not between us. You have to create the rotation by creating the proper connection with your right hand on my shoulder blade and your left hand with my right hand and step into the rotation. In order to look good you have to maintain your frame." I got it once. Then I could see it. It is all based on developing and maintaining a datum frame… just like making Matryoshka. I can see it because it is consistent with the models that are part of my life. I often make a cartoon of the moves because it helps me learn. Of course, the axis of rotation has to be her for this move, otherwise there is no balance. What fun to learn as I enter my 75th year.

Dancing has become a way of freeing my mind because all I can do is to think of the dance moves and how my body performs to the music. Those of us who are blessed with active minds need a way to divert them, to give them a rest, to allow us a moment of peace. Going from a wheelchair to dancing is a way for me to find peace, freedom, and wonder. I sometimes cannot believe I am still alive.

Dr. Raval, who is part of the team that saved my life, used to schedule his visits with me as the first patient of the day after I received a new heart. We usually started early. Even so, we often took too long and the administrator came in and told us to move along, as there were others waiting. We lost track of time talking about hearts and pumps, and drawing pump performance curves like the ones you learned about in earlier chapters. "Dr Raval, only God puts two positive displacement pumps in series."

"Maybe," he replied. "But He put a large compliance between them." The heart is the same as any pump. So the model of pump performance curves was a common language.

With every single project, the objective is to find the ultimate simplicity that is hidden, but will reveal itself with a sound strategy constrained by principles and proper models and proper questions.

I committed to writing this book and telling this story in such a way as to help you see the beauty and simplicity of the science of performance and reliability engineering. If you commit to learning the simplicity of how the physical world reveals its nature, you will be on the proper path. The world of tools, fishbone diagrams, and lists are not simple. Then again, perhaps they are too simple by half, and not proper when the problem really calls for Effective Characterization of **System Behavior**.

Data displays must be clear, assured, reliable, sturdy. In designing information, then, the idea is to use just noticeable differences, visual elements that make clear differences, but no more – contrasts that are definite, effective and minimal.

—Edward R. Tufte

Think of the stepper motor, where dogmatic application of tools led to confusion and frustration. Changing the question might just be the first step, not only in problem solving of machines but also in life as well.

Just as in life, the simplicity of the science of fixing things comes from principles, models, and constraints – not tools, or rigid roadmaps based on the application of those tools. When we construct models in life and in science, we make choices. Simplicity is not always obvious. We have to create it. It takes discipline and the ability to shut out the cacophony of those who seem to thrive on confusion – confusion that leads to the structure to manage it. Simplicity is not always easy; but simplicity is the only choice.

For most of you, to be an extraordinary problem solver you don't have much to learn. You already know it. Perhaps freeing your mind from dogma and learning a few simple models is all you need. Our mission is to show you how to take what you know, combine it with a few simple principles, and get on with it!

Once you learn to see – to understand how the physical world of performance and reliability reveals itself – you will become an extraordinary problem solver… and have fun doing it.

Mathematicians are only dealing with the structure of reasoning and they do not really care what they are talking about. They do not even need to know what they are talking about or as they themselves say, whether or not what they say is true.

—**Richard Feynman, The Character of Physical Law**

Chapter 10

The Role of Innovation

"We need a meeting to discuss the strategy."
"What is your strategy for this problem?"
We need a new business strategy."
"Our strategy is to reorganize to cut costs."

Strategy is never independent of structure, no matter the level of sophistication or the project. You cannot, or should not, think in terms of one without the other. Structure consists not only of capital equipment and buildings, but also the organization as well.

What you must know about strategy is the relationship to structure, and that the phase relationship is precarious and critical. Once you develop a strategy and put a structure into place to execute, the structure beyond the point of strategic initiation can quickly become flawed. In the midst of the current technical revolution it is not a matter of years, but could be weeks or months. Minimum structure with designed flexibility is the only way to stay effective in the midst of a revolution. Often, in an effort to meet strategic objectives in a time of stress, structure is expanded, which may impede innovation. Just as the relationship between strategy and structure must be kept in phase, so must the relationship between structure and innovation.

The history of war is a story of countries that were structurally prepared to fight the last war all over while the strategy of war changed. The structure for the last war impeded the innovation necessary for the next. The history of companies might not be as well studied; but the failures and near failures are a story of strategy, structure, and innovation breaking phase relationship.

When I was a young man, I worked for a company that made components and assemblies for computer hard drives. It was a thrilling learning experience in more ways than one. The business was new and we were engaged early. We thought we would all be rich in no time!

I was in my early 30s when I became the operations manager (yes, it was a long time ago), and I had little idea what I was doing. We were making 1 megabyte hard drives that were as big as a small washing machine, expensive to power, and selling for $40,000. Today you can buy a terabyte for a few dollars. I was learning to use VisiCalc before the days of Excel while making projections that were, in retrospect, silly. We bought machine tools and built tooling as if we would be able to sell all we could make for months, without a clue as to the technical breakthroughs an hour away. We no sooner had the plant up and running when innovation in storage capacity rendered what we were making junk. We were victims of Moore's Law, which says that computing power and storage capacity will double every two years. Moore was wrong. It doubled every year!

Strategy and structure were out of phase at a speed that stunned us all. We had done a good job of doing the wrong thing. We created innovative tooling to keep the spindles cutting metal. But with a bit more labor, and simpler machine tools and fixtures, we could have lasted longer. We were innovative, but wrong.

I learned a painful lesson about strategy and structure, but it took many more years before I could articulate it. It took time, experience, and study before I could write about the importance of strategy, structure, and innovation.

Strategy and Structure: Chapters in the History of the American Industrial Enterprise by Alfred Chandler was published in 1962. As a historian, not a management guru, he researched the strategic and structural evolution of four companies: Dupont, General Motors, Standard Oil, and Sears Roebuck. Each was a pillar of American capitalism. The growth of these companies became important to American enterprise. These were companies that grew as they served markets not accessible prior to railroads, rapid communications, shipping, disbursed manufacturing centers, and supply chains. They had to figure out how, and build the structure to meet the strategy, without impeding innovation.

Sergio Caredda reviewed and summarized Chandler's book, and identified four sequential stages:

1. Acquisition of resources such as employees and materials, and the buildup of marketing and distribution
2. Establishment of functional structures to increase efficiency
3. Adoption of growth and diversification strategy – diversification into new markets, and products to overcome limits of home markets
4. Creation of the then revolutionary divisional form to manage large conglomerates

Even though published in 1962, his summary is still important. I think Caredda left out a critical element of Chandler:

Initial strategy always breaks phase relationship with strategy. Once this happens, structure may well impede strategy. *The risk is that the structure drives the strategy, not the other way around!*

The structural strains caused by a new strategy often impede strategic execution. During the period Chandler studied, company size and market domination allowed for caution and measured responses. Change took time not available today.

No one should be surprised by the new industrial revolution we are engaged in today, but Chandler knew the basic foundation required to thrive. According to Chandler, organizational innovation is the key to keeping strategy and structure from breaking phase to the point of failure. In older organizations, he says, the expansion of legacy departments is often the antithesis of innovation. Older departments may expand the structure in order to perpetuate their own existence, garnering power to do so from higher and higher levels. Such departments become monuments.

I would argue that General Electric is an example where the structure drove the strategy when Jack Welch, among other things, defined the company as a Six Sigma company. Kodak defined itself as a company that made film and cameras and built the structure to do so. One of their employees, Steve Sasson, invented the digital camera. Leadership took no interest as it was judged a threat to the existing structure. Structure drove the strategy, and innovation was discouraged. Sasson is in the engineering hall of fame. Kodak is gone.

Contrast that with Stellantis, an interesting company that combined Chrysler, Fiat, and Peugeot, three companies from three countries and cultures. Stellantis no longer defines itself as an automotive company but rather an Electronic Mobility Company. The strategy is clear, and suitable for the times.

The Role of Innovation

If you choose to buy a copy of *Strategy and Structure* by Chandler, I suggest you include a copy of *How Innovation Works and Why It Flourishes in Freedom* by Matt Ridley.

Ridley studied the relationship between invention and innovation. He investigated steam engines, turbines, the telegraph, wireless communications, transistors, computers, and more. In almost every case, one person owns a patent. Ridley reveals that it was a race to the patent office to be first, with one example of a patent filing taking place two hours before a disappointed competitor. Behind the story of invention is a greater story of innovation, with many contributing while one person owns the patent. With such inventions as the steam engine and the turbine, the patent owners built machines of little practical value because of poor efficiency. England was the first to use coal-fired steam engines, and the first to fill the air with dense smog.

It was the freedom to innovate that provided machines that were of practical value, leading to efficient engines that power our economy, transport our goods, and give us the freedom to move around. Important inventions were a function of timing and technical application. The Wright brothers were credited with the first sustained flight. They were innovators who had invented nothing!

The point Ridley wants to drive home is that innovation does not get the same credit as invention, but that innovation makes inventions practical. The real game is innovation!

Ridley claims in *How Innovation Works*, "Big companies are bad at innovating, because they are too bureaucratic, have too big a vested interest in the status quo…"

From the lessons of Hadley in *Strategy and Structure*, we learn to think in terms of the integration of strategy and structure and maintaining phase relationship, remaining wary of how structure drives strategy when broken. From Ridley in *How Innovation Works*, we learn the relationship between structure and innovation. Neither works without the other.

That means that strategy, structure, and innovation are intertwined. Maybe it could be better stated that they must be carefully integrated.

Structure, Innovation, and Quality

There is no doubt that emphasizing the importance of quality has made substantial improvements in goods and services over the last 50 years. Quality has become an integral part of organizational structure, without which demanding strategic goals cannot be met.

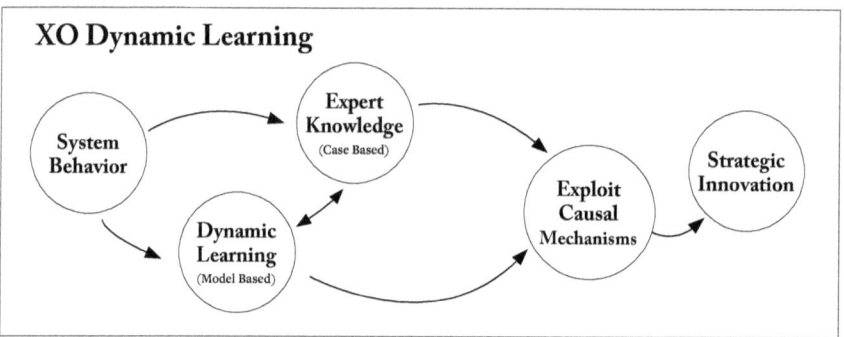

FIGURE 10-1

I submit that in many companies today, the structure for quality has broken phase with the strategy. In some companies, the structure of quality has grown to the degree that the strategic objective of quality departments is to perpetuate its existence. Goals are colored belts, progressive levels of certification, and seminars to teach tools – not strategy-centered product performance and reliability, grounded in **First Principles**. Training often starts with a large pool of candidates in seminars, then progresses through several certification levels with the *last man standing* certified as some sort of master or the blackest belt. The very nature of such a program requires massive structure.

Ridley claims that outsiders can help with innovation. Procter & Gamble learned that it could not efficiently invent its own way to new products. The choice was to add structure or look to the outside. P&G, while looking outside, knew that in order to meet its strategic objectives, it was important to keep the outsiders from becoming part of the internal structure.

I think the **XO Dynamic Learning** model is a simple way to provide those in technical disciplines the ability to strive toward innovation.

It simply states that we must start with **System Behavior**, then foster a learning environment while engaging experts to gain insight and understanding as to how things really work based on functional decomposition of machine behavior.

Now let me tell you a secret. There is not one concept in this book, not a single one, that we invented. Everything in this book is because we are good students, and have studied the history of science and played a role. We were able to see what has been done by others and turn it into a means to characterize **System Behavior** *in an innovative way. We know that innovation thrives in freedom.*

I am grateful for the opportunity to write this book for you.

Thank you.

John

The Purpose of Knowledge as Action, not Knowledge

—Aristotle

Acknowledgments

A huge thank you to the many technicians and engineers from around the world whom I have worked with and learned from. It is because of you that David Hartshorne, Tobias Mack, and I were able to challenge the models of conventional problem solving and develop the new principles of decomposing System Behavior and Dynamic Learning. Thank you for the opportunity to tell the stories we lived together.

I am also grateful to Rod MacIntyre and Michael Forhan for merging our company into Crossover Solutions.

None of this would be possible without the transplant team doctors at Advent Health in Orlando, Florida, who saved my life, and the heart donor who lost his life and saved mine. I am especially grateful to Anita, Heather, and Zamarys. I would not have lived without the encouragement of Sam, Barbara, Lucille, Bill, Elaine, and Antonieta.

This book would not be what it is without the help of April O'Leary and Heather Davis Desrocher of O'Leary Publishing. They showed me how to write this story from the heart… the new one.

A genius prospers, not by deconstructing intricate complexities, but by exploiting unrecognized simplicities.

—Andy Benoit

Appendix

Characterizing a Garage Door Opener

This is a simple example of **System Behavior** for a common device. The important lesson is that every system is a series of functions connected together; and each function can either be identified and characterized independently or grouped with adjacent functions to simplify the model as necessary.

For example, the function of an electric motor is to Convert Energy from volts and amps into torque and angular velocity. There is at least one other function in the magnetic domain that we acknowledge but leave out. The losses are not ignored. We know that every energy conversion is paired with a transmission, where accrued losses (Z) are accounted for.

With any system, be it simple or complex, we start with a sketch or cartoon to help us see with fresh eyes.

There is a button attached to a wall with wires, or one in the car that operates by a radio frequency signal. Either way, a relay shuts that supplies volts and amps to a motor on a bracket attached to the ceiling. The motor shaft is hooked to a worm gear in a gearbox that rotates a sprocket. Volts and amps are converted to torque and angular velocity at a gearbox, to a shaft, then a sprocket.

Over the sprocket travels a chain, the ends of which are attached to a bracket and a lever to pull and lift the door. The torque and angular velocity are converted to force and (linear) velocity, thus pulling the door horizontally with the chain, with the vertical section of the door following along.

Garage Door

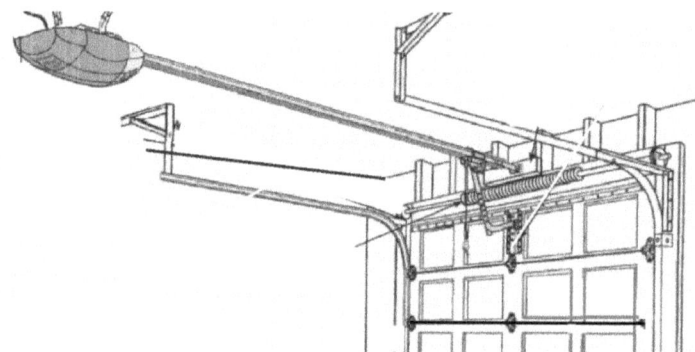

Figure 1

I live in Florida. The garage doors are reinforced so they are hurricane resistant. Some people who have never been in a hurricane call them *hurricane proof*. Nothing is hurricane proof. But bottom line, the doors are heavy. The motor would have to be massive to safely lift and lower the door, but for a clever system of springs that stores energy when the door is lowered, and releases it when raised. It is simple and clever.

Once the door is open, the door contains Potential Energy as a function of its mass and height from the floor. Once it is lowered and released, that energy is stored in the torsion springs by winding them up through a system of cables and pulleys. Potential Energy is then stored in the torsion springs as the door is lowered, and released as it is raised. This is a clever innovation. If we get the balance just right, the job of the motor is much easier. Ideally, the motor would just pull the door along the horizontal section of the track while the spring does the vertical lifting

We seek a simple way to characterize and understand **System Behavior** before we attempt to figure out what is wrong with anything. As I have said many times, history teaches us that science is asking the proper questions and taking the steps to get meaningful answers. **System Behavior** poses two questions:

- How is this supposed to work?
- How well does it work?

Let's have a look at how we might simply sketch this out – but first, let's start with a bit of an introduction.

Universal Source Load Model

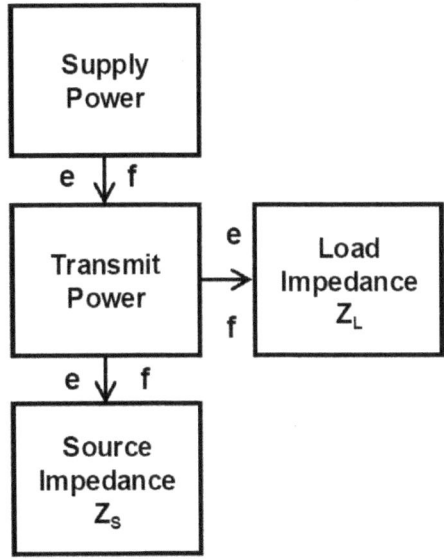

Figure 2

E-FAST – Conjugate Variables, Energy, and Power

The building block is the **Universal Source-Load** model in Figure 1. It simply states that in order to make a machine function, you have to have a source of power to supply a load. The Power Supply requires two variables called conjugates because they work as a pair. One is the Effort variable and the other is the flow variable. The flow variable is units per second. Multiplying the two together yields power in watts or joules per second.

Supplied power is split in two in the universal model. The load losses are called load impedance. We also want to know the story of the losses during the transmission and conversions between the supply and the load, or source impedance.

The **Universal Source-Load** model simply accounts for the fact that when you supply power to a machine, there are losses along the way. The model not only gives us the ability for a summary, but also allows us to see what is happening in:

- an instant of time within a cycle
- a cycle
- as the load changes
- or as performance decays, a precursor to failure

Decomposing behavior in such a manner imbeds **Matryoshka-Small Multiples** into the **Source-Load** model.

As we characterize **System Behavior** with the **Source-Load** model, we can group adjacent functions without ignoring them, which is consistent with the **Sparsity of Effects** principle. The idea is to gain insight and understanding while keeping the model effective, telling the entire story without unnecessary and confusing details.

Decomposing the Garage Door Opener

The motor converts volts and amps supplied by a wire plugged into the wall into torque and angular velocity as the output shaft rotates.

Convert Power, Electrical to Rotational

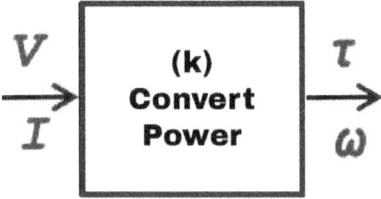

FIGURE 3

There are two variables, the combination of which are needed to describe what is called an **Energetic Function**. The electric motor, supplied by volts, draws a current in amps based on the load. The motor conversion is to torque and angular velocity at the shaft.

There is another conversion at the sprocket from torque and angular velocity to force and velocity in the chain, which lifts the door.

Convert Power, Rotational to Translational

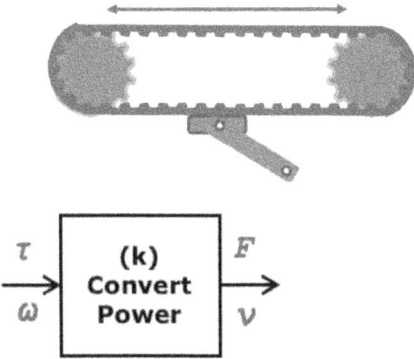

FIGURE 4

Whenever there is an energy conversion from one domain to another, there is a single arrow in, and another out, that represents the flow of power. There is typically a conversion coefficient in parenthesis inside the box, which is a multiplier to make the conversion from one domain to another. If we don't know what the multiplier is at the beginning of an investigation, we might cheat and write (k) just to acknowledge that we know there is one. (You can take measurements later to back into the conversion factor.)

The arrow labels are the conjugate variables described earlier. The label on top of the arrow represents the effort variable, the bottom the flow variable.

Effort-Flow Universal Conversion Model

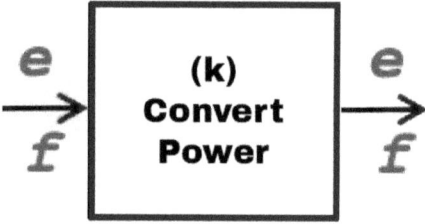

Figure 5

Every conversion function must be paired with a transmission (but not every transmission is paired with a conversion). Transmissions are where we account for the losses.

The International System of Units (SI) is used to keep it simple and consistent.

The table below shows the conversions you need to think through the garage door. Given that the effort × flow is watts no matter the domain, the last column is watts, so the losses along the way are easy to calculate.

Selected Domains and Units, SI

Domain	Effort	Flow	e × f
Electrical	EMF, V or E	Amps, I	Watts
Rotational	Torque, Nm	Radians/sec	Watts
Translational	Force	Velocity	Watts
Hydraulic	Pressure N-m^{-2}	m^3 sec^{-1}	Watts

TABLE 6

If you choose to be proficient, then learn to describe **System Behavior**. It is not difficult, and will only take a bit of practice. The time you spend practicing is the time you will not spend testing things that do not matter. **System Behavior** is the basis for engineering excellence with problem solving playing a role in the discovery process.

We all must build on the simplicity of what is possible and how it structurally fits, not only into organizational excellence, but also superiority that only comes from innovation, a function of **Dynamic Learning**.

I am not an expert in garage doors or openers. I don't want to be! Any list I might make of what might be wrong with a garage door opener would begin and end with a trip to the hardware store to buy a tube of grease or a can of lubricant. If there is a problem beyond a noise in the tracks, I would call an expert. However, in the factories we run and the products we sell, we need a way to gain insight and understanding that leads to knowledge of **System Behavior**. We need a way to learn fast and effectively in a world of ever more complex **System Behavior**. We not only need to grow and foster experts, but also a model for rapid learning founded on **First Principles**. Understanding **System Behavior** rooted in energetic interchanges is simple, and precisely what we need for learning machine behavior. Focusing on **System Behavior** must be the new role of quality engineering professionals.

The building blocks in the previous figures can be connected as necessary, with certain functions grouped while expanding the model as necessary to give a full picture.

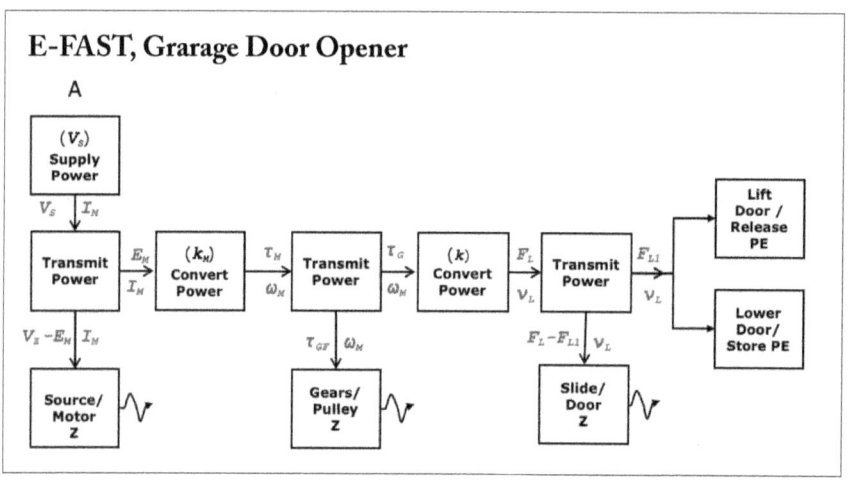

FIGURE 7

To complete the model, it was necessary to add the Contain and Release Potential Energy (PE) function based on the spring. Once again, as the door is lowered, PE is stored in the spring, and released as it goes up, helping the motor and keeping the motor load balanced. If the spring does its job, then most of the energy to lift the door comes from the spring and all the motor has to do is effectively position it along the rails. In the best case, the spring does all the lifting.

A Deeper Look

The motor is plugged into the outlet, which is 120 volts. Although the power supply is 120 volts, that's not what is available to lift the door. The motor resistance, which is mainly the windings, drops the voltage as the inductive field is created to spin the rotor, creating the torque. There are, of course, heat losses, grouped into Dissipate Power for simplicity.

Tranmit Power, Motor, with Impedance

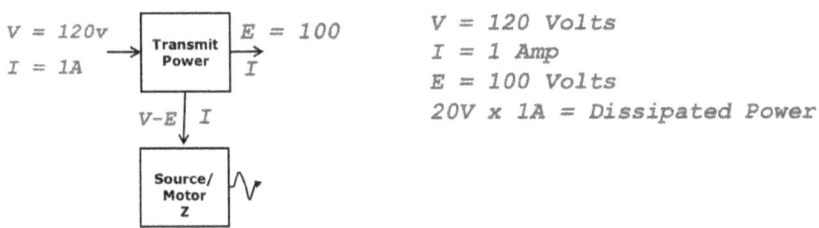

FIGURE 8

The supplied voltage is 120 volts. E is the common term for what is left over after the motor losses. I estimated (guessed) E at 80 percent of V, which isn't far off. The motor draws about 120 watts, and 20 are lost to source impedance, leaving 100 watts for the load. I don't have a current probe handy, but I looked up the motor current, which is about 1 amp depending on the load. I was surprised that such a heavy door could operate with a 1 amp motor – but we know it is because of the energy stored and released in the springs – as well as the gear ratios that make the job easier.

I checked the door with my iPhone. It took 14.56 seconds to lower and 14.61 to lift the door. I rounded to 15 seconds. The door has to travel 2.5 meters, or 0.2 meters per second.

I did not have all of this at my disposal and had to figure it out or look it up, which is easy today. By spending just a bit of time looking up fundamentals, you will give yourself a chance to make **System Behavior** the foundation for characterizing **System Behavior**, getting a proper feel for how something is supposed to work before you make an attempt to figure out what is wrong.

Between the motor shaft turns a worm gear. In a gearbox, the domain does not change. What changes is the ratio between torque and velocity with the multiplier shown as (k). The motor rotates at 1800 RPMs, or 200 radians per second with a low torque. The worm gear slows down the speed to the appropriate level for the sprocket to rotate in order to pull the chain back and forth that is attached to the bracket on the door. The torque and velocity of the motor is reduced through the worm gear and sprocket in the gear box, then converted to force and velocity at the chain to lift the door. Given the motor voltage and speed and theoretical current, and the mass of the door and velocity, the balance of the calculations are simple.

As the door closes, and the spring winds up and stores energy, it keeps the door from closing dangerously fast and pulling on the motor. If the door weighs 100 kg, then by the time the door is closed, each of the two springs will be loaded to release that energy as the door is raised.

Electrical to Rotational

Convert Power, Electrical to Rotational with Units

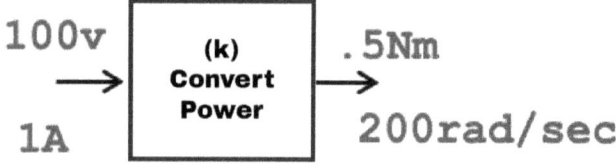

FIGURE 9

Given the angular velocity of the motor it is simple to calculate the torque given an estimate of the current.

We know that motor torque (effort) would be split during transmission between source and load impedances, while the velocity would be constant.

As we develop the full story of **System Behavior**, we have the flexibility to group functions based on **Sparsity of Effects**. There is also no rule that makes us work from left to right. Although we would start with Supply Power on the left, in this case we know the mass and velocity of the door as well as knowing it must be balanced by springs.

E-FAST with Flow of Power

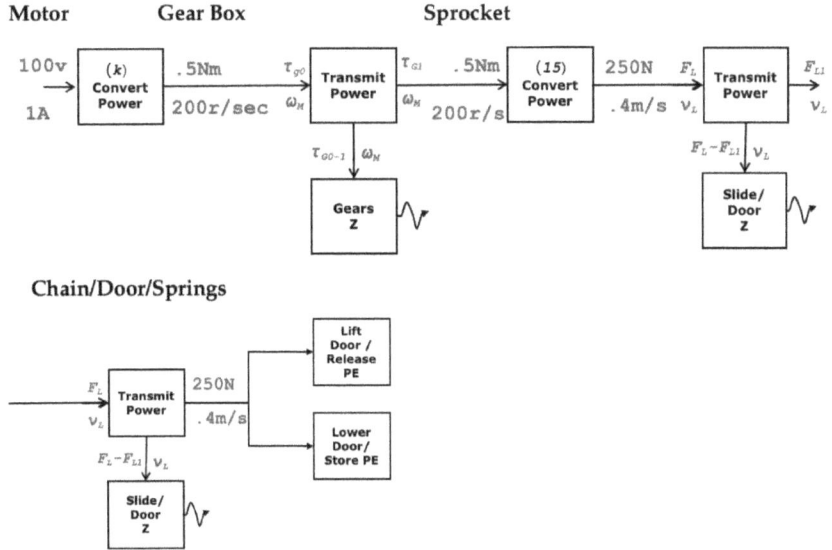

FIGURE 10

There is a worm gear on the motor shaft. We have to get the motor angular velocity from 200 radians per second to .4m per second of the door, and the motor torque from .5 nm to a proper force, which I found to be 200 Newtons. Using 33 for gear box conversion ratio and 15 for the sprocket or chain leaves 250 Newtons force with the velocity of .4m per second. The force is a bit higher than what is theoretically needed to lift the door, leaving a bit of margin for the losses.

Figure 10 also takes into consideration the torsion springs, with a *Contain and Release Potential Energy* function. This is quite clever as it takes advantage of the mass of the door and gravity to contain potential energy as it is lowered and stored, then release potential energy as it is raised, easing the load on the motor. I did finally buy a current probe, and discovered the motor drew the same amperage going up and down, meaning the system is balanced nicely by the springs.

Summary

The E-FAST is a functional map of functions with conversions and losses in transmission. It can be updated as we learn more about **System Behavior** and certainly a foundation for a powerful knowledge-capture system.

Once we have developed the E-FAST we can have a look at a single cycle, which is one opening and one closing, to get a pretty good idea how the entire system performs.

Simply measuring the current and voltage includes every function in the E-FAST. If any function decays, the current will increase.

Summary of the important lessons of this chapter:

- Learn how something is supposed to work before you try to figure out what's wrong. In other words, think in terms of Source-Load, not Black Box.
- Characterizing System Behavior with E-FAST gives you the ability to provide a Causal Explanation, rather than just a root cause.
- Causal Explanation is the key to competitive advantage and innovation.
- E-FAST provides a powerful communication device as well as a basis for knowledge capture.
- E-FAST is an excellent foundation for FMEA.

- How do we put the model to use beyond problem solving?
- A training model
- Functional model before FMEA to identify at-risk functions, not just failure modes
- A model to test new systems, and periodically throughout life

The development of the diagram of the model in Figure 7, called E-FAST, is the model we find useful for dynamic learning when we decompose a system into its energetic functions.

The fundamental functions of many of the machines we use today are the same as when invented hundreds of years ago. Continuous improvement and reducing variation of manufactured parts of poor designs did not get us where we are today. What did was innovation, which occurs at the intersection of **Expert Knowledge** and model-based **Dynamic Learning** based on improving **System Behavior**… and no other way.

Data displays must be clear, assured, reliable, sturdy. In designing information, then, the idea is to use just noticeable differences, visual elements that make clear differences, but no more contrasts that are definite, effective and minimal.

—Edward R. Tufte

Glossary

Aggregation
The combination of multiple sets of entities or data into a smaller number of groups. Time-series presentation of data is extremely sensitive to aggregation (choice of intervals and start-end points).

Analysis of Variance
The procedure of subdividing variation with respect to different explanatory variables. Also called *ANOVA*.

ANOVA
 See *Analysis of Variance*.

Average Range
The average of individual subgroup ranges.

Cartoon
A simple sketch to capture manufacturing machine-part interface and datum scheme.

Case-based Reasoning, Strategy
Diagnosis by reference to symptom-cause relationships previously established. See *Symptomatic Knowledge, Strategy*.

Causal Explanation, Mechanism
Causality is usually ascribed in light of what is normal for the situation.
https://fyx-z.com/2020/02/10/root-cause-or-causal-explanation/

Characterize
Map the behavior of product or process systems.

Cognitive Process
Human processing of information and application of knowledge.

Confounding
The grouping of input levels in an experiment, or omnibus factors in stratified sampling, in order to reduce the total experiment or sample size. If confounded factors have leverageable effect, additional tests or samples are required to separate the confounded effects.

Contrast
(Noun) In the context of analysis, an observation made comparing at least two elements where *reproducibility* or *repeatability* are of concern. For

example, measurement of *geometry* or *properties* at different points on a *feature* or performance differences of replicated systems. In the context of *DOE*, it is the difference between average output at varying input levels.

Correlation
The strength and direction of a linear relationship between two variables.

Data Map
Graphic relating locations and event occurrences to see concentration patterns. Also called Concentration Plot, Picasso Plot.

Deduction
One of three separate reasoning processes, deduction is to draw exact conclusions from facts, and check the effectiveness of a question *a priori*, whatever the answer. What will I learn if I do this test? What will I do next? See *Abduction, Induction*.

Dependent Variable
A variable being measured, also known as *response variable, responding variable, explained variable*.

Deterministic Model
Is one that produces the same output for a given starting condition. No randomness is involved in predicting future states of the system.

Diagnosis
The process of explaining machine behavior in terms of the geometry and properties of its constituent parts. Diagnosis is the inverse of *simulation*.

Discriminate
Distinguish, differentiate for comparative analysis.

DMAICR
From the Six Sigma methodology for process improvement. Each letter stands for one of the six steps in the process: define, measure, analyze, improve, control, and report.

DOE
Design of Experiment. See *Experimental Design*.

Dynamic Learning
A strategic process to learn quickly based on *System Behavior* and *Functional Decomposition*.

Effect to Cause Strategy
Also called Y to X, this is the overall approach of working backward from the observed performance behavior of a system to identify the geometry and/or properties with the greatest leverage or influence on that behavior.

Experimental Design
The design of an information-gathering exercise to establish the effect at different input levels of some process or intervention (the treatment) on objects (the experimental units).

Expert System
An expert system, also known as a knowledge-based system, is a database that contains some of the subject-specific knowledge, and contains the symptom-cause knowledge of human experts.

Families of Variation
Families are *Contrasts* or *Hierarchical* levels employed in the *Matryoshka* tactics. Structural families fall into two main groups: individual component *topography* and either manufacturing or operating system *topography*. Functional families must be defined by working from the output back to the input. The strata, or layers of data, are often called Families of Variation because each represents many variables or Xs.

FAST
Function Analysis Systems Technique. A top-down decomposition in which the functions of a product or process are described using blocks that state sub-functions using simple verb-noun logic, and the interdependency logic of these functions are shown in both the how and why directions.

Fault Tree Analysis
An undesired effect is written as the top event of a tree of logic. Each situation that could cause that effect is added to the tree as a series of logic expressions, using conventional logic gate symbols. When individual situations are assigned values for occurrence probabilities, it is possible to calculate the failure probability.

Feature
An elemental part of an object, such as a plane, a cylindrical surface, an axis, or a profile.

Forensic Evidence
Trace evidence used in an investigation (forensic means associated with legal justice), but used here in the context of machine failure.

Full-factorial Experiment
A full-factorial design of experiment (DOE) measures the response of every possible combination of factors and factor levels. These responses are analyzed to provide information about every main effect and every interaction effect. A full-factorial DOE is practical when fewer than five factors are being investigated.

Functional Decomposition
Dividing the overall function of a system into sub-functions that describe the how-why logic for achieving the system function. This is done hierarchically, with each function being further subdivided into three to six sub-functions at each level.

Functional Dimension, Feature
A dimension that is essential to the function of an object or space. A feature that is essential to the performance or serviceability of the object of which it is a part. It may be a location feature (e.g., a spigot that serves to locate a component in an assembly) or a working surface (e.g., a bore of a bearing).

Gage R & R
Amount of variability induced in measurements coming from the measurement system itself, compared to the total variability observed, to determine the viability of the measurement system. There are two aspects of a Gauge R & R: *Repeatability* and *Reproducibility* (see separate entries).

Geometric Tolerance
Specification that defines the allowable variation for the form and possibly the size of individual features, or the allowable variation in orientation and location between features.

Histogram
Graphic used to relate proportions of populations to single variable. A graphical description of the distribution of data, primarily used for summarizing. Can be used qualitatively.

Hypothesis
A suggested explanation for a phenomenon. A progressive search is a series of alternative hypotheses starting with very broad and progressing to narrower explanations.

Independent Variable
Those variables that dependent variables respond to are called independent.

Interaction Effect
In statistics, an interaction is a term in a probabilistic model in which the effect of two or more variables is not simply additive.

Interdependent Variables
Variables involved in an interaction effect. Two or more variables have a (multiplying) effect upon one another's causal relationship with the dependent variable.

Isolation Strategy, Tactics
The tactics of the Isolation strategy analyze a system as a function with inputs, and tests to see which has the greatest leverage over the output.

Isoplot™

Isoplot™ is a trademark of Red X Technologies and is a Youden plot with the 95th percentile envelope of repeatability variation superimposed on the graphic.

Matryoshka Strategy, Tactics

The tactics of the Matryoshka Strategy decompose a system into its hierarchical levels, either functionally or structurally. Matryoshka can be used to identify leverageable contrasts and/or patterns early in a project.

Model-Based

See *Topographic*.

Multivari Plot

Multivari plots (Leonard Seder, 1950) are an example of *Small Multiples* good for displaying *Matryoshka* results graphically.

Novel Problem

Where we are unable to diagnose a cause from the symptoms (*Symptomatic, Case-Based Reasoning*) because we have inadequate case history knowledge, the problems are referred to as novel.

Occum's Razor

A principle stating that the explanation of any phenomenon should make as few assumptions as possible, eliminating, or "shaving off," those that make no difference in the observable predictions of the explanatory *hypothesis* or theory.

Paired Data Plot

Graphic used to show dependence/independence between sets of associated values, the range in both X and Y directions, and concentrations of results. Often used qualitatively with curves showing X-Y relationships. Also called *Scatter Plot*.

Pareto Distribution, Plot

A power law probability distribution that coincides with many types of observable phenomena in which an equilibrium is found in the distribution of the "small" to the "large." Sizes of sand particles are Pareto distributed, for example.

Picasso Plot

See *Data Map*.

Poke and Hope

Hypothesis testing *not* based upon a *Progressive Search*.

Polar Plot

Two-dimensional data map in which each point on a plane is determined by an angle and a distance. Especially useful in situations where the relationship between two points is most easily expressed in terms of angles and distance. The two polar coordinates are usually called r (the radial coordinate) and θ (the angular coordinate). r and θ can be converted

to the Cartesian coordinates x and y by using the trigonometric functions sine and cosine:
$x = r \cos\theta, y = r \sin\theta$

PPM
A measure of defective products; parts (defective) per million (produced).

Probabilistic Model
Causal explanation expressed as likelihoods of potential events occurring, and likelihoods of the underlying mechanisms of systems working in the manner we describe. An element of randomness is thus involved in predicting future states of a system.

Property
The functional response of a system, sub-system, or component to a source of energy. There are three classes of property of importance; inertance, compliance, and resistance. Specific properties depend upon the energy domain of interest; mechanical, hydraulic, electrical, etc. For example, compliance in the electrical domain is capacitance; in the mechanical domain it is stiffness.

Repeatability
The ability of a whole system, or sub-system, to provide consistent results. The variability from that system.

Reproducibility
Variability between systems or subsystems.

Reversible Function
Any function that can be reversed and repeated. In manufacturing, many assembly and measurement functions are reversible.

Root Cause
If a root cause is eliminated or corrected we can prevent problem occurrence.

Scatter Plot
Graphic used to show dependence/independence between sets of associated values, the range in both X and Y directions, and concentrations of results. Often used qualitatively with curves showing X-Y relationships. Also called *Paired Data Plot*.

Simulation
The process of using models to determine machine behavior from the geometry and properties of its constituent parts. Models may be mathematical (virtual) or physical prototypes. Simulation is the inverse of *diagnosis*.

Small Multiple
Graphic showing *Data Maps*, *Time Series Plots*, *Histograms*, or *Paired Data Plots* (and combinations of these) repeated for one or more *families of variation*.

Spatial
Data organized with respect to a reference (datum) in space.

Statistically Designed Experiments
Information-gathering exercises to establish the effect of some process or intervention (the *treatment*) on objects (the *experimental units*) are greatly improved by adhering to some important design principles that are statistical in nature, because of the presence of reproducibility and repeatability variation.

Strategy
A convergent diagnostic strategy is the plan for managing the acquisition of information in a systematic manner to explain machine behavior. Diagnostic strategies are essentially the way we model and decompose the models of the systems. Strategies are independent of specific information-gathering tactics.

Stratify
Stratification is the process of grouping members of a sample into homogeneous subgroups or *families*.

Structural Decomposition
Hierarchical division of a system into sub-systems or elements based upon what the system is made up from, or machines that it is manufactured by.

System Behavior
The sum total of a machine's ability to effectively and efficiently perform its intended functions throughout its expected lifetime.

Tactic
Convergent diagnostic tactics are the specific tests carried out to obtain data, and the analytic method used to evaluate the data to generate explanation.

Temporal
Data organized in time sequence.

Time Series Plot
Collect data sequentially, plot Y values against time on the X axis, and compare each reported value to the rest. Time-series presentation of data is extremely sensitive to choice of intervals and start-end points. Suffers from the weakness that chronology is not a causal explanation.

Tool
A technique for organizing, displaying, and/or analyzing data into information in order to answer a diagnostic tactical question.

Topographic Strategy
Model-based approach to diagnosis, developing *causal explanation* from basic principles. Most effective when applied as a *hierarchical decomposition,* either *structural* or *functional.*

Trial and Error
Hypothesis testing *not* based upon a *Progressive Search.*

Youden plot
Paired Data Plot in which the axes of the plot are "square" – same data ranges and same physical dimensions on the x and y axes. Two sets of results for any function repeated on the same sample of product are paired up, one on each axis. Function repeatability is manifested as the distribution of points perpendicular to the 45 degree line, *not* parallel to either axis as in a regression.

Bibliography

Alder, Ken, *The Measure of All Things,* Simon & Schuster, 2003

Bak, Per, *How Nature Works,* Copernicus, 1996

Bliss, Corinne Demas, *The Littlest Matryoshka Doll,* Disney, 1999

Bolles, Edmund Blair, *Galileo's Commandment,* Library of Congress, 1997

Box, E. P., J. Stuart Hunter, and William G. Hunter, *Statistics for Experimenters,* Wiley, 2005

Brown, Forbes T., *Engineering System Dynamics,* CRC Press, 2007

Bytheway, Charles W., *FAST Creativity and Innovation,* J. Ross, 2006

Clayton, Aubrey, *Bernoulli's Fallacy: Statistical Fallacy in the Crisis of Modern Science,* Columbia University Press, 2021

Dorner, Dietrich, *The Logic of Failure,* Perseus Books, 1996

Feynman, Richard, *The Character of Physical Law,* MIT Press, 1965

Goodrich, Clarence Leon, and Frank Arthur Stanley, *Accurate Tool Work,* Hill Publishing Co., 1908

Gordon, J. E. E., *Structures, or Why Things Don't Fall Down,* Penguin Books, 1991

Hamming, Richard W., *The Art of Doing Science and Engineering: Learning to Learn,* CRC Press, 2020

Hartshorne, David J., *Diagnosing Performance and Reliability,* 2019

Hill, Donald, *A History of Engineering in Classical and Medieval Times,* Barnes & Noble Books, 1984

Hindle, Brooke and Steven Lubar, *Engines of Change,* Smithsonian, 1986

Lightman, Alan, *Great Ideas in Physics,* McGraw Hill, 2000

Michelin, Francois, *And Why Not? The Human Person at the Heart of Business*, Acton Institute, 2003 (a gift from Bryan Ziegler)

Mlodinow, Leonard, *Feynam's Rainbow*, Warner Books, 2003

Ott, Ellis R., *Process Quality Control*, McGraw Hill, 1975

Reston, Jr., James, *Galileo*, HarperCollins, 1994

Richter, Jean Paul, *The Notebooks of Leonardo Da Vinci, Vol. 1*, Dover Books, 1970

Ricks, Thomas E., *First Principles*, HarperCollins, 2020

Ridley, Matt, *How Innovation Works*, HarperCollins, 2020

Ronan, Colin A., *Science: It's History and Development Among the World's Cultures*, Hamlyn Publishing, 1982

Rybczynski, Witold, *One Good Turn*, Scribner, 2000

Seder, Len, *Diagnosing with Diagrams*, Industrial Quality Control, Parts 1 and 2, 1950

Shapin, Steven, *The Scientific Revolution*, The University of Chicago Press, 1996

Smith, Daniel, *How to Think Like Da Vinci*, MJF Books, 2015

Smith, Merritt Roe, *Harpers Ferry Armory and the New Technology*, Cornell University, 1977

Tufte, Edward R., *Seeing with Fresh Eyes*, Graphics Press LLC, 2020

Tufte, Edward R., *Visual Explanations*, Graphics Press LLC, 1997

About the Author

John Allen is a clever problem solver with a reputation for quickly fixing complex problems in manufacturing and product performance. John was a founding member of Shainin LLC, and the co-creator of The New Science of Fixing Things, which merged with Crossover Solutions, an international consultancy, in 2022. In his 50 years of solving problems on *planes, trains, and in automobiles*, across the globe, John has worked with Fortune 500 clients as well as small companies. John received a heart transplant, the Gift of Life, on September 25, 2017, and does his best to live a grateful life. He believes it is his role in life to help others where he can, not just while solving problems. He lives in Naples, Florida.

www.ingramcontent.com/pod-product-compliance
Lightning Source LLC
Chambersburg PA
CBHW040251090526
44586CB00041B/2750